Simon →

Many thanks for your support

How To SUCCESSFULLY INVEST IN PROPERTY

by Mike Woods

Mike

First published 2014

CONTENTS

About the Author

I think it is important that I start off by introducing myself and also give you some details about my background; why I am qualified to help you to invest in property and build your portfolio. I have a genuine passion for teaching people how to invest in property and I hope that by telling you a little bit about my journey so far, it will inspire you to get started in property.

I was born in February 1964 in Bolton, Manchester. At the age of 5 my parents moved to Llanelli in South Wales, this was quite a shock! Can you imagine what it was like for a little boy with a strong Lancashire accent moving into an area with a strong Welsh accent!

My parents were licensees and took over a new pub for the area brewery. Due to their success when the brewery opened a new pub in a new area, they had my parents open it and get the business up and running. They were the perfect hosts.

When I was young this moving around every 5 years or so was unsettling, I never really established any long term friendships. In hindsight, whilst this was an issue for me at the time, the various moves have proved useful.

During my youth I was a rugby fanatic and would never be seen without a rugby ball in my hands and my talent as a rugby player became apparent from the age of 14 where I was selected to play for the regional schools team. At the age of 16, at the end of my 'O' Levels, we moved from Porthcawl, a sea- side resort in South Wales and we took over a newly renovated pub in a town called Loughor, on the border between Swansea and Llanelli. The issue for me was where I was going to play rugby? For me there was only one choice- Llanelli RFC, 'The Scarlets' the best team in the World. Fortunately from our earlier time in Llanelli, my father being well known in the area said that he would speak to someone he knew, a fellow publican who at one time played for the 'Scarlets'.

The next thing I knew I'm in the car with my dad going to see the coach for Llanelli Youth, who welcomed me to the team. A few years later at the age of 19 I was selected to play for the Welsh Youth, I am proud to say that I went on to play for Swansea RFC in the mid 80's alongside some immensely talented boys, who played for Wales, England and the British Lions.

So, what happened next? Well, the game changed from amateur to Professional and it was decision time, do I pursue a professional rugby career or one in the Construction Industry? You see, whilst I had been playing rugby I was studying Building Studies and Architecture at Swansea Institute of Higher Education.

I had decided that, in all honesty, compared to the quality of the players I had played with, I realised I didn't have that certain 'edge' needed to a professional rugby player, so I focused on my career in Architecture.

I gained employment as soon as I'd finished my first full time course. Again, call it coincidence, (which I no longer believe in, by the way) one day in Swansea I bumped into one of my old school friend's father from Porthcawl, I had a vague recollection that he was an Architect! Me being me, I immediately asked him if it were possible to have some work experience over the summer holidays.

The following September I enrolled on a day release course and was offered a job at his Architect's practice on the strength of me offering to work there for nothing over the summer holidays. The fact that the other partner was a Swansea RFC rugby fanatic and I was a Welsh Youth International, helped a bit I think! Ironically, a number of years later I played my first game for Swansea RFC and after the match, in the bar he was proud to tell his friends, that just a few year prior he had given me a job!

Over the next 10 years I worked for a number of Architects building up my knowledge and pay rate, and by 1995 I held a senior position in a large practice and began to seek a position as an associate or a Partner in the Swansea Office. It was apparent that the door was closed to me, because, I was told 'I wasn't qualified' so rather than take the money and be stuck in the role that I felt I was more worthy of, in August 1995 I tendered my resignation. A Month later I established my own Architectural Practice, I called it Concept Architectural Services and rented a small cupboard with a window big enough to accommodate a desk and a drawing board. I had been earning £16,000 a year gross, so my business plan was to get £16,000 of new business. As it turned out I did £32,000 in the first year. Within 4 years I had 3 staff and moved twice to bigger offices and was turning over £150,000.

In 1989 I got married and on January 1st 1995 my son Ben was born so the pressure was on to provide for my family. Unfortunately I didn't have the full support and understanding of my wife at the time and in October 1998 I found myself back in the bedroom that I once had as a teenager living with my parents; we had agreed to separate amicably and in the interest of Ben my son, I agreed that they would live in our house until such time it was sold and she had found another suitable house.

All that I had worked for the past 4 years had just evaporated. It's a really strange feeling that you are dedicated to the future of your family and the ground from below you collapses. I had a beautiful 4 bedroom house a 3ltr Toyota Supra, money in my pocket, she had her own car, and we had great holidays. All Gone! (except the car I managed to keep that).

To cap it all, my father, who I adored died suddenly of a heart attack the following year, not a good time, I was devastated.

Whilst my mother loved having her son back at home, I had to get my 'stuff' together and started looking for a house for myself, strangely I never considered renting. At the time I was still financially tied to the matrimonial house mortgage, but could afford from my income a small 2 bedroom link house in a small estate. My mother was tearful at the reality of me down scaling 'after all my hard work' she said, but it was a new start and an important one, as I was determined to rise up.

I paid £29,000 for the house and whilst I was doing my numbers learned that they were renting for £350 per month. The quick minded of you will have realised that this in rental terms produces a yield of 14%, so as soon as I could muster up a few grand I looked to buy my first rental, which happened to be next door! Within a few more months I had bought another house just around the corner.

I must introduce to you at this point to my first property mentor, a vastly experienced and street wise man called Billy Griffiths. He had started buying rental property in the 60's and by the time I met him had over 150 properties - he was a typical entrepreneur, owing a double glazing business and building companies. He had asked me to design a small site of houses and basically we hit it off and we have spent many hours together over the years socially discussing property and every aspect of life in general, he was instrumental in my success as he taught me the ins and outs of what to buy, where and what not to buy. Billy was always available and loved to see me grow. He playfully reminds me that my success is down to him.... and he is correct, it is. He is also my daughters Godfather.

In February 2001 I met my wife, Syvona and later that year I went to Africa to climb Mt Kilimanjaro raising money for the charity Whizz Kidz. Syvona and I got on really well, but it was funny as we would meet up after work for dinner at our favourite Indian Restaurant and she'd say, "Oh I bought a lovely pair of shoes today"! And I would say, "Oh I bought a great house".

As we had come together, both as 'business' people, she had a Beautician business, we didn't need to answer to each other financially and we still don't. One sunny afternoon in the summer of 2003, I was visiting a client just outside Cardiff and after the meeting I called her to say I'd be a little later than planned as I was popping into Cardiff. She immediately caught on, "You're not going to buy a Porsche are you" she exclaimed! Needless to say I did, the first of many. And she enjoyed driving them.

As we began to settle down, I was offered a parcel of land from a business acquaintance, more than big enough for 3 houses in the

Brecon Beacons National Park, I agreed to buy it to design and build a house for us and build out the other plots and sell them on. I actually managed to get 4 plots on the land so without him asking, I paid the vendor for the extra plot. Some people would not have considered doing this, but I strongly believe that 'what goes around, comes around' and that you should treat people with the same respect that you would like to receive.

The next few years were busy and planned meticulously, we started the build in 2004, at the same time we were organising our wedding in Florence, Tuscany by flying out there every few weeks ready for the big day on the 4th November 2004. I remember the date well; Wales were playing the All Blacks in Cardiff.

We moved into the house in February 2005 and our daughter Maddison was born on the 9th of May. And to cap it off in November I won the 2005 Daily Telegraph and Home & Renovation Magazine 'Self Build' Award for our house.

By the financial crash of 2007 I had amassed a portfolio of over 20 houses. I had designed, built, bought, refurbished, let and sold more.

The period after the financial crash was initially very worrying, after such prolific activity everything just stopped, my architect's office phone stopped ringing, I even called the office number from my mobile to check it wasn't a fault with the line. I would continue to meet with my mentor Billy and the word was that the banks were calling in overdrafts, some of us had racked up huge overdrafts based on our cash flow and depending where you were in a phase you may have just sold a house and the money was in the bank or due in, whereas it could all be out invested in a house or two being refurbished. If it were all out you had a problem as people stopped buying and you were unable to re-mortgage.

The banks decided they wanted to recover all the unsecured debt, we were all very worried. The Banks at the time were running scared, the banking system was in chaos! We all got called in and their offer was to restructure the overdrafts to loans over 3 to 5 years and charging us hefty fees and higher interest rates. Of course publicly they were making out that they were lending money, business as usual! They had been loaned millions by the Government and told to lend it, but they weren't, they were securing their own positions and filling their Black holes.

So fast forward to 2013, I'd been ticking along doing refurbs and the odd new build, but due to the changes in the benefit system and limited availability of mortgages HMO's were becoming more popular, so I purchased a few suitable properties and converted some of my single lets using my own funds. Life was good and I had much of what we needed, but I had an urge to do something else. Something BIG. I was 49 and I needed a new challenge.

A friend told me about the Power to Achieve (P2A) event in London run by Andy Harrington, my friend said that he had taken his 21 year old son and it was of help to him to realise that there were no limits to one's potential so I thought it would be of benefit to Ben and decided to go, Ben was 18 at the time and from what I had heard I knew he'd love the block breaking and bar bending as he was into martial arts. Little did I know how much effect this event would have, on my life.

It was at this event that I met Kevin Green, I knew of him of course, being Welsh and local to me, and had seen him on the Channel 4 program 'The Secret Millionaire', but had never heard him speak. It was here that I decided that he was the man who could help me take my business forward I felt that we sung off the same sheet and I recognised similar core values. You see, having done what I had over the years and being the only person I know who had 40 plus rental properties (other than Billy) you're unable to measure yourself, if that makes sense! But Kevin said something that weekend that stuck a cord with me, he said that when he had Interviewed Sir Richard Branson, he had told him that 'if you recognise qualities in someone that you respect, then that is who you are'.

I enrolled on the Kevin Green Wealth 3 day Advanced Property and

Business training and during the 3rd day of the course ask for a few minutes of his time, he is a very astute man and has a knack of being able to suss you out in seconds. So I simply wrote on my pad my age, the number of houses in my property portfolio and my qualifications, then asked him, "what can you do for me" ?

We had a conversation about what he could do and how the coaching program would help me, so at that event on the 9th January I enrolled on the Kevin Green Wealth 90 day Coaching and on the 16th January I attended a meeting with Kevin and my appointed coach Dan Latto. At this meeting we set a number of objectives, to which I was accountable for and needed to have monthly meetings with Dan to report on my progress. One objective was to create a brand for myself, speaking and training and to become a coach. In addition Kevin said that I should be a Welsh Assembly Government Role Model and he would contact someone who he dealt with to recommend me.

I immediately started work on my objectives and got on with my life in general. In February I got a call from Big Ideas Wales, the WAG section that is responsible for selecting Business Entrepreneurs as Role Models to go into schools, colleges and universities and provide inspiration to young people. Following an interview and attending an induction course I received a letter confirming my appointment. In addition I had received an invitation to become a Prince's Trust Business Mentor and following a 2 day induction course received a letter of appointment. I was now a Welsh Assembly Government Role Model and a Prince's Trust Mentor! Amazing.

On the 16th March the call came from Mr Green, some coaching clients wanted some property input in my locality and asked if I would like to assist. Of course I accepted and following a successful meeting I received an email from Kevin simply saying 'Welcome to the coaching team'. The next chapter in my life had begun.

Those of you who have been on Kevin's Property and Business Training will have heard him refer to his 'clearer' friend Sandi. Kevin is very spiritual, and having spoken to Sandi since being involved with Kevin it turns out that prior to his call to me he had Sandi 'check me out'. Fortunately I did not need clearing and in her words 'I'm one of the good guys', which was nice to hear.

In June at the Kevin Green Wealth 3 day Property and Business training course held in Bristol, Kevin asked me do a one hour talk on any property subject matter. I chose to do a talk about Homes of Multiple Occupation- HMO's that I titled 'How to PLAN your HMO'.

In my introduction from the stage I use part of this story to impress upon people that in order to make change you must take action, Anthony Robbins will say 'Massive Action'. For me it was attending the P2A event, meeting Kevin and making a decision to ask Kevin to be my Mentor.

From this, and having nearly 30 years in Property experience, I am now a Kevin Green Wealth Coach, coaching people to make a difference in their lives, training people in Property and Business and helping young people in colleges and universities on behalf of Big Idea's Wales by giving inspirational talks and mentoring young business people for the Princes Trust. How good is that?

I would never have thought in November 2013 at the P2A event that any of this was possible. Having Kevin as my Mentor has changed my life completely and I am very excited about my future; you don't know what opportunities lie ahead unless you are open to change and are prepared to take action.

Kevin has offered the following advice, which I hope you will appreciate.

"Self-awareness is the Master Key to Success, Achieving Clarity of vision through self-awareness opens the door to endless possibilities".

Kevin Green Wealth Coach and C4 'Secret Millionaire'.

www.kevingreen.co.uk

I have now established my own Mentoring Program under the Brand 'Mike Woods The Property Expert', where I offer Personal Mentoring to individuals who want to fast track their property learning experience, avoid making costly mistakes and getting straight into earning money from property such that they can consider leaving 'employment' and become financially independent. I will also be holding Property and Refurbishment Master Classes, which will be held in venues around the country.

Go to: **www.mikewoodsthepropertyexpert.com** for further details. Please leave your details and your property goals and I will personally get back to you.

CHAPTER 1

How to Successfully Invest In Property

Chapter 1. How to Successfully Invest In Property

What this book can do for you.

In a nutshell, help you to make money, change your working life and give you financial independence by teaching you how to Successfully Invest in Property, but not only that, it will help to save you from making costly mistakes that can lose you a small fortune either by buying the wrong property in the wrong area or wasting money because you don't have the right knowledge.

Please note and I stress 'Successfully Invest In Property' you can go off and start dabbling in property, it is fraught with danger. There are people out there who have been in property two minutes and will try to sell you training courses, offer to find you property (in the wrong places, in my opinion) and invite you to joint venture, by asking you for a load of money up front, so be careful. Not all that Glitters is Gold.

My aim here is to share with you my experience, as I believe knowledge is one of the keys to success, and show you how to get started. Whilst I don't like to be seen to be bragging, I've done very well out of property over the last 25 years. Perhaps the fact that I started out in the Architectural business in 1986 means that I have a head start on many as not only do I know how to construct a property, I can de- construct them. That is, I know how they are put together, so I know how I can take them apart economically. I can fix them because I know how or why they are defective.

Through surveying hundreds of properties in order to extend them, convert the attic or lofts to create another room in the roof, convert a damp basement into a teenager's or granny suite, convert or extend a garage to create a granny flat, I have learnt an awful lot about different types of properties and construction methods.

I have also converted old derelict barns into modern spacious homes; over the years, when I think back I've had the pleasure and honour of creating some great new homes for many families to live in.

There are many books out there on the subject of property investment and letting, but it seems they don't cater for the ordinary person such as yourself who wants to make a small business in property without having a huge pot of money available; after all who has these days?

But before we get started I felt it would be important for you to understand why the property business is where it is today, why property prices are what they are, why property is so investable and why the availability of mortgages are what they are, so, please read on.

UK House Price History

According to the Halifax, the average UK house cost £2,507 in 1959. Fifty years later, a typical home would set you back £162,000. In other words, the typical house today costs almost 65 times as much as it did 50 years ago. Put another way, over 50 years, the typical house has grown in value by 8.7% per year.

However, both wages and the cost of living have increased dramatically over the same period. After stripping out retail price inflation (RPI; the rising cost of living), the Halifax reckons that house prices have risen in 'real' terms by 273% since 1959. This equates to a more modest growth rate of 2.7% per year.

But put it like this - if your parents bought 4 properties in 1960 for £10,000 and rented them out they would have received a constantly increasing rent for the past fifty years and if they sold them all tomorrow they would be retiring on a healthy profit.

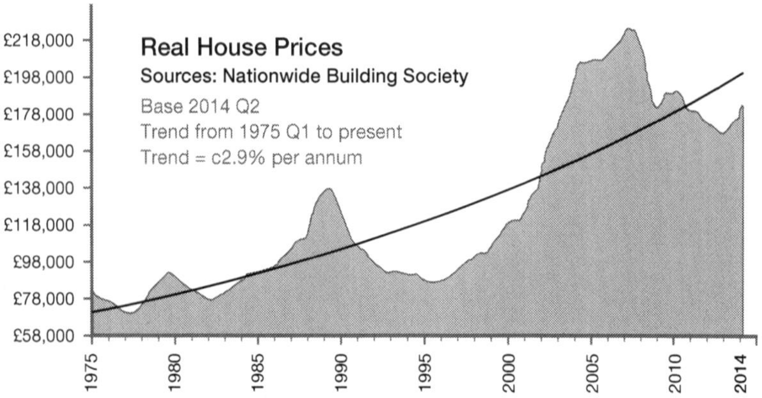

They would have probably taken out a 25 year mortgage, so the mortgage would have been paid off in the mid 80's. The rent received since then, unless they re-mortgaged would have been pure profit, less of course any maintenance costs and any voids. But, Overall a good Investment, No? Had they re-mortgaged (leveraged), they could have reinvested those funds to buy more, and more over the following years.

The Property Boom for UK property prices really took off in early 2000. The chart above shows that previously there was a increase in trend that started in 1996, but in 2000 the market really heated up and then, after more than a decade-long boom, the market peaked in late summer/autumn 2007, and then prices tumbled as banks beat a hasty retreat from easy lending. House price falls accelerated through 2008 and property market activity hit record lows in late 2008 and early 2009.

By December 2007, the Halifax index said the average home had fallen by 18.9 per cent.

Whilst this is a dramatic fall let's not forget to see the big picture. For those who have been investing in property since the 1980's and 90's, property prices had risen by over 200% (in some areas) in the ten years to December 2007. I did not intend on selling or need to sell so for me the drop in house prices was a disappointment, it was great seeing your net worth going up, a real 'feel good' factor, so personally I was not overly concerned. But some I knew were very concerned and started off-loading, why I don't know, probably they over-paid and were over-geared, and of course they were in some cases not able to cover the mortgage and folded.

You see in every rising market there is a period before the peak called 'the winners curse', that phase when there's a mad rush before the doors close. Where every man and his dog were buying property as house prices were rising weekly, but when it all crashed so did the inexperienced.

The UK property market was in what is referred to as a 'Bubble' and a perfect storm hit the UK property market in 2008.

The problem was the housing market was out of control, the availability of credit and apparent constant rise of property prices gave people confidence to get credit and secure huge debt against their home or BTL property, the more properties you had the more confident you were.

Fortunately, I was positioned in one of the main areas in the UK where property prices were increasing rapidly. In the 12 months to October 2004 the average house price increase in Wales was 37%; in my patch, Swansea and Neath Port Talbot, the records show an increase of 42%. In real terms the 20 or so houses I had by then in those towns had risen from £30,000 on average to £43,000 in 12 months.

Taken from the book titled 'Boom Bust' by Fred Harrison, Henry Trick the property commentator of the Financial Times reporting on house prices announced 'I am hanging my columnist boots and throwing my estate agent' brochures in the bin. Why? Because I can no longer claim to have a clue what's going on in the housing market'.

The Credit Crunch

The pin that burst the bubble was the credit crunch. The sub-prime crisis that had been brewing in the United States erupted in the summer of 2007, and as the year continued, the residential mortgage-backed securities market that had driven massive growth in credit for home loans essentially ceased to exist.

So, what happened? To briefly explain, we need to go back a bit. In the US, banks and financial institutions devised discounted mortgage products to encourage families to get on the housing ladder; these families were people who would not have ordinarily been able to access the housing market, Sub-Prime was the name given to them. They were sold the American dream and offered to take cheap loans and mortgages on the assumption that they could rely on the rising house prices and that they would always have collateral in their homes. They were then offered other loans to fund cars and holidays etc. but when the Federal Reserve increased interest rates to cool down spending, (the spending that the banks had encouraged by lending cheap money) thousands of these sub-prime home owners started to default, which in turn caused house prices to fall. This then undermined the value of the 'products' on which the banks traded between themselves.

These Investment products were packaged up by lenders with sub-prime (high risk) and non sub-prime (low risk). Fees were taken from the outset and these investment packages were sold to other banks and financial institutions around the world, for more fees, and used as security for pensions plans and the like.

When the sub-prime home owners defaulted on their payments the bankers and financial institutions realised the implications for the value of the investment 'products' (the pension plans). Investors around the world panicked and looked to sell the investments, which in turn reduced their value, and as nobody wanted to buy these 'hot potatoes' their value tumbled, leaving completely innocent investors around the world high and dry.

It wasn't long before the big US banks started to panic and this started to include the UK banks. It became apparent that many, including massive banking institutions such as Lehman Brothers, had massive 'black holes' in their accounts. They were insolvent and filed for bankruptcy on 15th September 2008. The banks went to the Federal Reserve Bank of New York for support but the Reserve felt that lessons needed to be learnt and did not offer what became known as a 'bail out'. In the UK the same had happened, but the Government felt that had HBOS, Lloyds and RBS not received support the whole banking system in the UK would have collapsed.

For more information go to **www.publications.parliament.uk**

'Boom Bust' by Fred Harrison provides an in depth explanation of the events leading up to and of the Depression of 2010, he lays the blame squarely on the politicians of the day both in UK and the US. This brought about the collapse of Northern Rock; within 4 weeks of the Credit Crunch in the US, Northern Rock was for sale. You may recall the news in the UK showing queues of people outside Northern Rock banks wanting to take their money out; over 4 days depositors withdrew approximately £3bn, despite offers of reassurance from the Bank of England. The British public did not trust the Government and withdrew their life savings in cash.

The banks became scared, they stopped lending even between themselves let alone to the consumers. With credit drying up Interest rates rising, Money 'the oil that lubricates the world economies' dried up and the whole thing came to a grinding halt, Overnight.

Banks fearful of huge losses examined their own 'black holes' and began to dramatically cut back on mortgage lending and a vicious circle began. The more banks cut back on lending and raised deposits to deter people from applying for loans, fewer homebuyers could secure finance, as the availability of credit dried up the more property prices fell and banks became more fearful and cut back further on lending. And the rest...is History.

What I find Ironic about this and leads me to think that the people who run the banks were clueless, is that the at the end of the day the result of the tightening of lending, which came about from their unregulated over lending and skulduggery, the banks have ended up with a massive stock of properties which they have repossessed, which in turn have dropped in value, due to their continued actions or inaction, whichever the way you look at.

The Mortgage Crunch

Mortgages are the key to the property market. The vast majority of buyers cannot purchase a property without a mortgage and the availability and restrictions imposed on these have the biggest impact on their ability to buy a property.

The slump in property prices in 2008 came as lenders withdrew from mortgage lending, with some specialist Buy to Let Lenders like Mortgage Express, closing their books to further lending. Some continued but decided that they would stop lending on apartments and flats in new developments. Those in the business then saw new marina developments and blocks around docks etc. being put on hold and sites being mothballed. People had placed a deposit on the apartment in the hope that they would continue to rise in value, were looking at all ways of trying to get out of the deal, including me I hasten to add. I had committed to buy a £285,000 apartment on the Swansea Sea front, at the time 85% mortgages were available. 18 months later, when the apartment was complete, the best I could get was a 60% deal, that meant I had to find £114,000 as opposed to £38,700. I managed to delay the completion by preparing a defects list, which took the contractors 5 months to rectify.

The main sticking point for the contractors was the issue of safety glass. You see, all glass adjacent to doors, in doors and in windows below 800mm must be safety glass and all safety glass must be identified as such by carrying a British Standard Kite Mark, usually in the corner. I noted that none of the glass in the apartment had the required markings. So I requested that they provide me with proof that the glass was indeed safety glass. Why they were not appropriately marked remains a mystery but In the meantime I found a buyer to take my place. I sold the apartment for £276,000, and lost £9000 on the deal! You can't win them all.

Those lenders that remained in the market raised the level of deposits required from 15% to as much as 40%, some lenders were pulling mortgage offers at the eleventh hour or offered alternative/ unattractive products to deter borrowers from taking up the offer.

Some, in order to avoid lending or to instantly change the LTV figures were telling their surveyors to undervalue a property, which resulted in the buyer having to stump up more 'deposit' at the last minute or pull out. In other cases people were in the middle of purchasing a property and waiting for a mortgage offer, which never arrived. These actions by the lenders threw the market into chaos.

The Bank of England's monthly figures also showed mortgage activity simply dried up in what seems like overnight. Mortgage Express prior to the crash had a monthly magazine issued to customers, which included surveys of their clients' portfolios and their views on the future of BTL markets; this magazine was produced to market their products to investors and landlords, encouraging lending.

Prior to the crash my lenders would regularly write to me saying that their 'index' shows that my properties have gone up in value by 15-20% in just 6 months and would offer me further advances with no fees. I was regularly pulling anywhere between £8,000 and £12,000 out of each house.

One lender, which I won't name, got it so wrong, and before the interest rates started to tumble offered me a 0.5% BELOW base rate tracker. So when rates finally fell to 0.5%, they wrote to me saying that their system won't accept 0% interest rate and that they must insert a value into their system so they used 0.001%. I had three mortgages at the time totalling £250,000 and I was repaying 6 pence on each per month. This was a two-year product. Happy days! A quarter of a million pounds of credit effectively interest free for 2 years. I often wonder if the bright spark in that bank kept his or her job after crunching the numbers on that product.

My point here is that the Men and Women in blue pin-stripe suits didn't have a clue what was going on; this bubble was surely never going to last, it simply couldn't, it was unsustainable. But the powers that be, the people in the City just didn't see it coming, they didn't want to, as they were receiving huge bonuses.

Moving On - Supply and Demand

Pessimists would have had you believe that property in the UK was doomed, but that ignored the fact that houses are not like stocks and shares. They don't go up and down daily or weekly depending on whether your MD took out a City fund manager for an expensive lunch.

In 2007 just before the crash, a 'weekly money' publication (the name of which I won't mention) recommended that 'you get out of property now'. Fortunately I didn't take any notice of this advice. I have never been one to follow the crowd, as this didn't any make sense to me whatsoever. My properties were renting and income was flowing, so why sell? As interest rates started to drop and drop, those with correctly geared property portfolios saw their profits rising, I personally started to see my monthly interest payment drop by over £2500, which meant I was 'making more money'. I often find that publications and their authors are very narrow-minded, and focus on London and then use this pattern of events to broad brush forecast what will happen around the rest of the UK.

A piece of advice I would give, is not to listen the news or take much notice of the press, these organisations need to produce news daily, they have to find something to report on, regardless. I have known different publications to have completely opposite reports, they are merely someone's point of view based on the data that they are seeing and how 'they' interpret it. It has been shown that in the years leading up to the crash of 2007, no one, and I mean no one, had ever experienced a property market like it was. All the journalists were making it up as they went along. So my advice would be to get educated, learn what you can and keep learning. And don't be pulled off course by people who don't know what they are talking about. Find a Mentor who can walk the walk, someone who has a proven track record and don't settle for less.

I was the owner of an Architectural Practice where the work just dried up as people didn't want plans drawn up to extend their houses or Plans to build a new home 1. Because they couldn't get the money form the banks and 2. Once people realised that their property was not rising in value, they stopped investing in it.

Had I not had my property portfolio, who knows what would have happened to me?

Mike's tip!

Don't believe all you read, make your own decisions. Get a Mentor that can walk the walk, this will help you avoid making mistakes, save you time and Ultimately help make you money.

While falling property prices have brought tough times for those who have seen equity slashed, fallen into negative equity or even had their homes repossessed, there are others who are pleased that prices were falling.

Demand for property in Britain always remains high, prices may had fallen by nearly 20% by 2008, but many potential buyers see this as a good purchasing opportunity. Ultimately, confidence returns to the market, In fact at the time of writing, London property prices have risen by 18% in the first half of 2014, a search of properties around the main commuter rail links to London show that everything under £200,000 is either sold or under offer.

The shortage of supply of property in the UK compared to demand has, arguably been exaggerated by developers and the Government, but decent sized family homes in popular areas are typically in short supply and property in areas of low unemployment will always see a high rental demand.

Over the last year or so, there has been a sharp rise in landlords diversifying and there has been a growth of a small army of new investors focusing on HMO's (Homes of Multiple Occupation) where houses are being modified such that a tenant can rent a room in a house where they share the bathroom and kitchen. Again though, this strategy is nothing new, I'm sure all of you reading this have seen or know of the television program 'Rising Damp' where Leonard Rossiter plays the role as Rigsby the landlord of an HMO, which was first aired in 1974.

For those who can secure a BTL mortgage and raise a deposit are in a very good position. We are currently still in a 'Buyers Market' this means that the 'Buyer' has the upper hand. However, as ever it always comes down to supply and demand and the demand is rising month on month across the country.

As you progress through this book and learn from my personal experience 'How to Successfully Invest in Property' you will become more aware of methods that will enable you to:

- Identify and buy properties at prices that will enable you to sell at a profit
- Learn how to identify properties that have the potential to be refurbished and sold on at a profit or re-mortgaged and still have money left over
- Re-circulate your funds
- Learn how to manage a refurbishment project
- Learn how to deal with tradesmen
- Learn how to purchase building materials at the right prices
- Learn how to identify a hot spot for your Buy to Let Portfolio

- Learn how to negotiate to ensure you pay the absolute minimum price
- Learn how to take control of a property without buying it –Lease Option
- Learn how to identify areas that you should avoid buying property in
- Learn how to maximize rental income
- Learn how to Minimize expenditure (and increase your profits)

There are experienced Investors who are purchasing property without putting any of their own money down, and own property with none of their own money left in.

Other investors including myself have been using various methods and buying property with other people's money, 'Joint Ventures' for years. I would recommend that you work with someone that you know and do not advertise for partners; by doing so you will not fall foul of the Financial Conduct Authority.

A Typical Joint Venture

In 2009 a retired Solicitor friend approached me to enquire whether I would be interested in working with him, his comment to me was 'he would rather make 50% of something than 100% of nothing'. He had been aware of my success in locating property for the bare minimum and getting them rented out quickly and releasing funds later. So he placed £100,000 on the table and we did the deal. He put in the money, I did the work and we split everything 50/50, ownership and profits.

I went out and within a month bought 2 properties, next door to each other in fact, which had been repossessed. They were both in need of a little work. It was apparent that the previous owner saw the writing on the wall and removed the boiler and bathroom fittings from one or the other. We bought the 2 properties for £82,000 and I spend a further £8,000 getting them ready to let. (Registered with the land Registry as tenants in common)

I had tenants occupying both houses within a month at £475 per month each. After four months we applied for mortgages, they both valued up at £65,000 and on the stroke of six months drew down 75% mortgages, which returned us £97,500 gross. £96,200 after legal fees. Needless to say my new partner was impressed, and was keen to see another two properties added to our new portfolio.

I repeated this exercise roughly every six months for four years, each time replenishing the pot, at which point a mutual friend a 'tired' landlord asked if we would be interested in buying a block of 3 flats for £80,000. My instant reaction and subsequent research found that these flats were easily worth £50,000 each. Once I had viewed them it was apparent that they were looking tired and needed modernizing, nothing major. The kitchens were from the 1970's and the place needed a complete freshen up.

We agreed to pay £80,000 and got my team in to embark on a minor refurbishment program, stripping out and replacing the kitchens, new tiling, respatex to the bathrooms, new carpet and re-decoration. I spent £18,000 from our pot. As the three flats were under one roof, a former large three storey house, under one title this leant itself to a commercial loan rather a Buy to Let mortgage. Once fully let which took about 4 weeks, the bank instructed the valuer and agreed to a gross valuation, steered by me by showing him examples of other flats in the area of similar size and circumstances of £150,000. We received funds from the bank of £105,000 gross, £103,500 net after arrangement fees and legals.

So, as we stand today we both have a 50/50 share in property portfolio worth £750,000 with gross rental income of £60,000 net. The stake money is still in the bank ready for the next deal.

I often have people approach me to do something similar, but I don't work with just anyone. I knew my partner for a few years before, and we have absolute trust in each other, the sort of trust that is difficult to explain, it's something you just instinctively feel. We have joint bank accounts that we both have online access to and if I want to pull £500 pocket money out, I ping him a text or email telling him I helped myself and ask him to do the same. He's quite funny as his replies are often...'that's jolly nice of you old chap. if I must'.

I'm not suggesting that in the early stages of your property journey that you will be able to do this, but if it inspires you to learn more, get yourself in a position of trust and respect with your peers, you may well find that they will ask to invest with you.

The Future

Now, if I had a crystal ball and was able to have a definitive forecast on property prices in the future I would be wealthier. But Alas, I nor any other person can be so certain.

However, let's take a moment to consider the past and here are a few thoughts:

Over many years the UK economy shows that there is a cycle of Rise and Fall every 18 years or so, also the Usury Law reduced interest rates in 1714 to 5%, and this by the way is the rate that the Bank of England currently considers to be the 'Neutral Interest rate' (5%).

The records will show that in the UK there have been recessions in 1776, 1794, 1812, 1830, 1848, 1866, 1884, 1902, 1920, 1938, 1956, 1974, 1992 and the latest in 2010.

The previous chart shows house prices rising to 1971/2, falling to 1974/76, rising to 1979/80, falling to 1982/83, rising again to 1989/90, falling to 1996 and lastly peaked in 2005/07, so a quick analysis shows that historically house prices rise between 8 to 15 years, I believe that 2004 should have been the peak and that in 2001 we should have had a recession, (like other EU countries) but Gordon Brown proudly managed to avoid a recession. He wanted to keep inflation to the target of 2.5%, but these figures did not include house price figures; had they done so, inflation would have rocketed. So, he encouraged the British public to spend their way out of a recession by giving tax breaks and reducing tax. We were set up for a inevitable massive crash.

No matter what the governments of the day do, no matter how much they tweak the interest rates and try to influence the economy, the property market seems to have a life of its own. Some property trainers will be heard to say that in the UK property prices double every 10 years. Records will show us that the average price of a property in 1977 was £13,000, in 1987 it had tripled to £44,000, by 1997 it has increased by 40% to £61,000, then by 2007 tripled to £180,000. In 2005 a more realistic figure of £157,000, still an increase of over 250%. The average price at the end of 2013 was £186,000 (20% increase).

The UK had been in the depth of recession for 4 years, a longer period than expected, figures were released and the Government prematurely announced that the UK was out of recession, only to see the quarterly figures drop us back in and talk of a double dip recession.

What seems apparent to me these days is that after such a long time in the doldrums, people have started to say 'enough is enough', their attitudes have changed and they are no longer prepared to put up any more and will make more of an effort to succeed.

So, where do we go from here?, People who are interested in investing in property have the faith that, unlike any other investment, probably because you can see it, touch it, smell it, go inside it, whatever way you experience it, it's a physical object and as Humans I believe we like to 'have things'. I love 'collecting' properties, it gives me a buzz, from the moment I get a call to going to see it, doing the 'deal', buying it, walking around it with the pride that 'this is mine', even when I find one for my wife, I 'present it to her with pride', 'here you are darling, come and see what I've found, do you want this'?

Unlike other Investments, even though the banks have been troublesome, you can still get a loan against the security of a property. There are now other 'crowd funding' groups to be found online who are offering quicker solutions to access funding.

Do I believe the guys who say property will increase every 10 years? Let's see, they peaked in 2007, so in order to double we should be seeing a peak again in 2017, just 3 years from now, so I doubt it. Will they go up again, yes most certainly. As mentioned London prices have shot up, but London has a life of its own with foreign investors pushing up the prices. This I feel will ripple out across the country. What I find is that where houses are on the market for a while and low offers can be made as the vendors become frustrated and want to sell for whatever reason, I am finding now that houses priced attractively are selling within 4-6 weeks.

If I am tasked to build someone a property portfolio in an area, whether it is local to me or in another area, when I do my research on a property I will look at the sold prices in 2005 as a realistic starting point.

If we use sold prices of 2005 and discount the false highs of 06 and 07, do I think they will be double in 2015-17 again, I'm not so sure.

So here is an exercise for you.

Search on Rightmove or Zoopla for a house or houses for sale in an area that you would or are considering investing in.

Then, Search for past sold prices by going to **www.nethouseprices.co.uk**, insert the post code and click the tab 'sold prices' in the filter which is set as default '3 years' change that 10 years. You may widen the search by typing the town or first 4 characters of the postcode, this will show you the streets in the area of your search.

You may well see that the house you are interested in or one that is for sale will show up as being sold in the last 10 years and the price it sold for. I often see that something is for sale now at a price below what it previously sold for, admittedly those tend to be the ones that were previously bought in 2006/7.

If you see something there below the price it was sold or bought for in 2005, then I would seriously consider it. Of course if it were massively cheaper in 05, it may have well been in need of modernization and has been improved. This process can really pull you in and you can find yourself searching for hours, but it will pay off in you saving £000's.

Now if you are interested in Buy to Let look at the average rental income rates. I wouldn't use net house prices for this as the average taken is over a wide area; simply search the local agents for monthly rental rates. And then use the calculation of gross annual rent divided by the purchase price to work your potential gross yield. Ideally you're looking for a figure that is around 8-10% or more.

CHAPTER 2

Getting Started

Chapter. 2 Getting Started

Without stating the obvious in order to invest in property you need to have some funds; I appreciate that there are many new strategies out there where you can get involved with rental property by way of 'rent to rent' and 'lease options', but you are not investing, you are earning some money from property. Investing to me is having a financial interest in the property, whether I am able to pull the deposit out or even more, my name is on the title of the property and its mine to do with what I want. I also appreciate that not everyone has got immediate access to funds, but again as I mentioned previously, if I can inspire you and get you excited about property then you will have had some value from this book.

Throughout this book I will provide you with real examples of my property journey from my personal experience to help you understand and perhaps formulate a way of your own, rather than give you strategies. By all means I do not profess to have all the answers and the way I do things may seem a bit scary or risky to the less adventurous. Since my involvement as a Wealth Coach with Kevin Green I have realised that many people aspire to have property portfolios, but find it a little daunting. To be fair we are dealing in many thousands of pounds, and if you get it wrong by buying the wrong property in the wrong area, you're stuck from the start.

So, hopefully my advice and examples will get you thinking; after all you don't need to re-invent the wheel.

But, don't fear that you are alone on your journey once having read through the book. If you want more guidance and support you can attend my 'Property and Refurbishment Master Class' which are held over a couple of days at various locations around the country, where we cover all the aspects of property investment and ensure that you are fully armed. In addition you can contact me directly and enrol on my Personal Mentorship Program where I will provide you with one-on-one support to fast track you on your journey. However places are limited, so don't delay for next year.

Details can be found at **www.mikewoodsthepropertyexpert.com**

Here is the first example to whet your appetite:

A few years ago I was talking to my mother who at the time was 64, she said that she had given the very nice man at Barclays £20,000 to invest for her 5 years prior and she had just received the cheque following the policy maturing. She was very confused, 'I gave him £20,000 and he assured me that this investment was a really good one, so good that he had invested in it himself" she said. Then told me that she has had received just £17,000!

"Why did you do that?" I said, 'I could have done better than that for you." Typically she said, "Well I know how busy you are with your properties, I didn't want to bother you. After all the very nice man in the pin-striped suit said it was a good investment plan"! Of course he did; at least you can recognise Dick Turpin!

So, I explained to her that if she gave me £15,000 I would find a property for her that would cost £60,000. Because of her age she would not be able to get a Buy to Let mortgage on her own, but together we could. Within a few weeks I found a really nice first floor flat in a block of two, ex-council where the ground rent and maintenance charges are usually very low.

The agents called me to say that the property was on for £66,000. I offered £58,000, which the vendor wasn't happy with and stated that he wanted at least £60,000. As it happened the flat also had a lovely large garage and he was using it for spraying cars and doing car repairs. As I needed a re-spray for my race car, I agreed to £60,000 if he sprayed my car for me; he agreed and the deal was done. He sprayed the car during the time it took for the solicitors to do their thing.

From my local knowledge I knew that I could achieve £390 PCM for the flat, it was in immaculate condition (the guy was a bit OCD), so no work to be carried out. I rented the flat out within 3 weeks. The monthly payment on the £45,000 loan was £180 PCM. Since the day we bought it my mother has pulled £150-160 per month out of the 'hole in wall'. The property was purchased as 'tenants in common' which means that we have an equal share. In the event that anything happened to her or me for that matter, each are able assign their interest to someone else. In her case probably my brother, in mine my wife or children. And we have not spent a penny on maintenance since as there has been no need.

I manage the rental aspect of the flat for her, and take no money. The asset value is always there for her to assign. Yes I have the other share, but as mentioned in chapter 1, 50% of something is better than 100% of nothing and in this case my mother gets 100% of the rental profits. Without me the deal wouldn't happen, I have the risk of the mortgage, but I'm sure you will have gathered by now I won't lose any sleep worrying about it.

What about the maintenance I hear you say, well yes, you would be correct the prudent ones amongst you should be putting 10% away every month. As mentioned the property was in excellent condition, the structure is maintained by the Council, as the ground floor flat in still in council ownership, the maintenance fee and ground rent is a massive £25 per month. And if anything did need to be done there I would send my guys around and sort it. Type of thing you do for your mum! Wouldn't you?

So, if you have a relation or relations sitting on a sum of money earning absolutely nothing or even less in the bank or have an endowment policy nearing maturity, consider teaming up, they put the money in, you do the work and split the money and the asset. Do this half a dozen times and you're on a roll. And you can still do this whilst you're in full time employment, you will have to spend a few hours in the evenings and weekends should you need to give a place a splash of paint, but in the beginning you've got to get things done yourself. I did, I have installed kitchens, laid laminate flooring and it's been known for me to have been seen with a paint brush in my hand, but not often. I absolutely hate painting, bores me to tears.

But where can you buy properties for £60,000? I have often heard this recently, and yes I agree, I am fortunate that I live in South

Wales and it is/was far easier to get started in the late 90's when I was buying properties for £20,000- 30,000. So, my advice would be as follows:

Research areas within an hour of where you live, closer if possible where the property prices are relative to the annual rents by a factor of 10-12. For example if you have identified that rents in a particular area are £5200 per year (£100/week) then you are looking for the prices of the houses to be around £52,000-£62,500. This will produce a gross yield of 8-10%, I appreciate that you will need to make allowances for maintenance and management etc, but it's a quick way for you to identify areas. I will go into detail later in the book to show how to work out Yields and Return on Investments.

If this isn't possible, then you will need to consider investing in another area. Through the Kevin Green Coaching I have met many people who are researching areas around the UK.

My recommendation would be:

- Identify an area that works in terms of rental demand and affordability
- Visit the area and get to know the Estate agents and the area
- Identify no go area's and don't invest there, every town has one
- Check out the earnings to house price ratio
- Once an area has been identified focus on it and look to build a portfolio of a minimum of 5 units.

The earnings to house price ratio is something that I and others have used to work out if an area in investable. We use a factor of 5. You find out what the average house price in an area is, from one or many of the house sales websites, Rightmove or Zoopla and then from the HMRC web site or Wikipedia find out what the average annual income is.

For example, if the average annual income is £20,000 using a factor 5 the average house prices for your chosen area should be £100,000. This we perceive as an area that the people can afford mortgages and rents.

Ot... r research you should carry out if you are focusing on lower priced property focuses on the fact that your property may be in an area where you could take private or LHA (Local Housing Authority) tenants. Tenants who seek assistance from the council to help with their rent -housing benefits.

Each Local Authority has a scale of housing benefit allowances, depending on the size of the property, who lives there and their ages.

For details go to: lha-direct.voa.gov.uk/search.aspx

I have readily taken on tenants in receipt of housing benefits, one of my longest term tenants has been with me for over 14 years. She has moved houses 3 times as her family circumstances have changed. I would say she is one of my best tenants. On the other hand I have rented houses out to people where I have thought they need a break or have come across as being very respectable only to have the place left in a mess when they leave or in one case trashed.

Another way of getting on the first rung, is by raising money from a loan or from credit cards. Whilst this may seem a little reckless, you must keep a tight control. You would be looking to raise funds from either or both sources, securing a loan for £10,000 from a bank loan or from a crowd funding organisation such a Funding Circle and some from a credit card provider that is offering 0% for 12-18 months will get you on the ladder. Yes, you will be paying a higher rate of interest early on, but in the big picture the sacrifice will be small. In Chapter 1 I referred to the fact that house prices in the UK rise, if you can get your portfolio going in 2 years or so, you will be glad you made every effort.

Here is another example,

At the time of writing, just 3 weeks prior I had a call from one of my estate agent contacts. It was a Friday at 12pm, a house that had been on the market and not on my radar at £70,000 had just been reduced to £60,000. The property was taken as part exchange by a national house builder and as it was nearing the end of the month and they need to hit their monthly figures, they had reduced it. I was asked how soon I could view it, I confirmed by 12.45pm. The house was immaculate, the only thing that I needed to do was fill in the holes on the lounge wall where the flat screen TV bracket was fixed. Being a little cheeky as I am, I offered £52,000; by 2pm the deal was done at £55,000.

I called into our office to tell my wife of my latest acquisition and asked her if she wanted to go halves with me, early on I used to keep my little bargains, as time went on I'd offer them to her for her to build up her own portfolio, then for tax reasons, I would suggest we put them in our joint portfolio. But on this occasion she said that we should give it to my little girl Maddison.

Maddison even only 9 is a little star, I'm bound to say that though. But honestly, a few years ago she started in a dance troupe in Swansea called Maniax, run by Makers Of Dance Energy- dance school. Maddison also started to go to a local stage school. In those short years, she appeared on the kids' Kindle Fire TV advert, she has been on a Harry Enfield sketch and she now appears on Sky 1's Welsh sitcom STELLA, with Ruth Jones and very recently was called to play a small part in the latest Dr Who with Peter Capaldi. Better known to me as Malcolm Tucker from the BBC's 'The Thick of it'. Tucker the F***ker

As a result of the TV work and birthday money she has accumulated just short of £5,000, so we agreed to 'match fund' and will make up the balance of £13,750 for the 25% deposit and we will open a separate bank account from which the mortgage will be paid. Of course Maddison at the age of 9 cannot get a BTL mortgage, so we will do that for her and once she is of age transfer the title to her. But the income from the rental will go to a dedicated account and will be left to accumulate. No doubt she will have a fair sum in the account by the time she really needs the money and by then the asset will have increased. I won't suggest a University fund because that's not my way of thinking, and if I'm honest I think she is destined for a bright entrepreneurial future.

But I'm sure you're thinking, that she is lucky little girl to my help and guidance. Well, here's the thing... You can have it too.

Estate Agents

So, how do you find these properties I hear you say?, Well the most obvious place initially is from Estate agents. So, let's look at what these people do.

They will get a call from a potential vendor, go out and appraise the property and advise them on how much they believe the house should go on the market for. I'm sure that you have seen the various Property programmes on the TV, and you will have noted that the estate agents who comment on what the house is worth or should go the market for always vary, and then often the sellers will generally disagree with the lower valuation and then opt to go with the company that advises on the higher valuation.

Well here's the thing, 95% of the sales will be in the area of the lower valuation, but the valuer who place the 'higher' valuation got the commission. You will find this is apparent throughout the country, no doubt you have seen a house for sale, it's been on the market for a while, and then there is a reduced marker on the board.

The agents that I deal with are the realistic ones, they are also the agent that have the lower sales fees. I have often mentioned that I had seen a house 'for sale' with another agent at an unrealistic price and the agents have told me that they had been out and valued it £5000-10000 lower, but didn't get the commission, only for the seller to come back to them when the original agents can't sell it for 6 months. Then they put it on for the price then recommended and 'hey presto' sold!

So, on the basis of what I have mentioned above, locate such an agent in your given area, and go to their office, often there is more than one in a postcode area, and introduce yourself but be honest and try to keep your ego in control. You're not the first 'big spender' or 'out of town investor' that has crossed their threshold. Be pleasant and keep it simple, 'you are looking to buy a property that you can refurbish and when it is complete you will be giving it back to them to sell for you', or 'you are looking for a house to Buy To Let'; ask if they have a lettings department, if they have mention that as you do not live in the area, you will be looking for a letting agent and you would be happy to speak to them.

Some years ago I was looking to purchase a little two bedroom terraced house which had a tenant, the agents were acting as letting agents for the owner. In order to position myself with the agent I promised that 'if' I were to buy the house that they could continue to act as letting agent for me. Needless to say I had the house, and still have.

They will prefer it that you are 'proceed-able' which means you have the money available, they will use the term 'a cash buyer', not that you will walk in with £50,000 in £20 notes in a plastic bag, it simply means that you will not be relying on a mortgage to purchase. Which in turn means that your purchase is not subject to you securing a mortgage on the property and because of this, the time to purchase the property will be quicker. Something that is often important to a seller- speed of the transaction.

If you do need to rely on funding to make the purchase, have your mortgage broker provide you with a letter showing that you have a 'decision in principle' from a lender, this is where you have made an application for funding to a lender, they have credit checked you and approved 'in principle' a level of credit. This will give confidence to the agent that you are 'proceed-able' and if they are negotiating with a vendor for you, they can confidently say that they have seen your 'financial position' and that you are bone fide.

Often agents will have an 'in house' mortgage broker, ask them during your initial enquiry if this is the case, perhaps say that you will need a mortgage and would it be possible to meet with their broker when you visit; if you do this the agency will get more fees, and will have a little more confidence with you as 'their' broker is handling the finances from you, they only need to make an in-house call or pop upstairs to check the progress of your mortgage.

When arranging viewings, always be prompt and on time; what you are looking to do ultimately is show them that you are reliable and serious about what you are doing. Be courteous and above all install a level of confidence with the agents. If the property is not right for you, say so immediately and be clear as to why, don't make positive noises in effort to be pleasant, often the person that opens the door for you will not be your main contact, the person at the house viewing will relay your comments back to the office. If those comments are positive and during the follow up call you start being negative with all the reasons why the property is not for you, they will wonder why you didn't say that at the time.

For me, I have always maintained a very high level of Integrity and honesty, I have 'never' not purchased something that I have agreed to following a viewing or even during a viewing. Subject to agreement of the price of course. Even then I have rarely not purchased something, as usually the reason I am at the house is because the agent has called me knowing that it fits my criteria for location and price, often the deal is done within an hour.

Throughout my career, I have ensured that that I do what I say I am going to do, even as a kid if I told my friends I would be somewhere at a certain time, I'd be there. My business colleagues and associates know me to be reliable. Just think of 'Ronseal - it does what it say on the tin.' If you can operate at this level you will not go far wrong. Don't 'over promise', it will only bite you in the bum and you will rapidly lose respect.

If you are successful with your purchase, don't disappear now you have what you wanted. Your purchase will take at least 4-6 weeks and your refurbishment project anything between another 4-12 weeks, depending on the extent of work and how you go about it. Once the agent issues the 'memorandum of agreement' to all parties contact your solicitor and notify them to expect it, call your mortgage broker immediately about the exciting news. Then call the agents, the person that you have been dealing with, not just anyone and leave a message. (You are rapport building, so try and deal with one person, and try to make it the most influential one in the office). Let them know that you have notified everyone and that you have asked them to proceed with haste.

If during the buying process the solicitor calls you with some information that may cause a delay, an anomaly with the land registry title or something, call the agents and let them know; they will be pleased that you are on the ball and see that you are taking action.

Once you have completed, they will call you and let you know that the keys are available for you. Take the time in the office to sit down and have a chat, let them know that you have enjoyed dealing with them and that you look forward to keeping in touch and that your will keep them updated on the progress of your refurbishment and let them know when it will be ready to go back on the market.

Having done all of that, I'm sure that you can see there is no reason why the agents will not call you in the future. But, you must remember in this day and age there are many such people as yourself in this business, so don't expect to be the first on the list.

Because of my long-standing relationships with agents, I am a 'regular customer' and invariably will get an early call, but I'm not always in a position to buy, or want to buy everything that comes my way. This is where my Master Class Mentees will benefit, I am perfectly happy and always have been to share my deals and nurture my clients to financial freedom.

Mike's tip!

When searching for properties do not be put off by something that does not initially appeal to you, try to look at it the objectively. You are not going to live there.

Options and Lease Options

Options

'Options' have traditionally been used by developers looking to secure a parcel of land or a building for their future expansion, speculating on the increase in future value. For example, a developer may identify a building or a parcel of land that is not currently being used or classified under Planning for the purpose they require, a farmers field for housing or a commercial building for apartments.

The developers will look to take out an 'option' to purchase the property at a later date, after they have ensured that they are able to do what they want with the property. The cost to the developer in these cases can be huge, Planning applications, Consultants and engineering fees, ground investigation reports and structural engineers reports. In order to protect their investment (the money that they are spending on the fees) they will look to enter into a written agreement with the vendor stating the price they have agreed to pay in the future and the timeframe to complete the purchase. The option agreement will also require the purchaser to pay an option fee, often 10% of the agreed future purchase price. This payment is normally non-refundable.

These agreements must be 'watertight' as when the purchaser has done all the hard work, over often a few years and expended thousands of pounds, the vendor may balk in the knowledge that the field he agreed to sell for £50,000 is now worth £4m and try and wriggle out of the option agreement.

The term for the above exercise of uplifting property values is known as 'Planning Gains' and can be massively lucrative, as you can see. A friend of mine who lives in London has been doing this for a few years, he identifies houses with overly large gardens, or small workshops or mechanics garages in residential areas, establishes the value of a new house in that street, calculates what the cost of the house would be to build including all fees (the GDC- Gross

Development Costs), makes an allowance for an element of profits, and the balance is what he is prepared to pay for the land. If he feels that this would be attractive to the building owner he will write them a letter making them an offer under the terms of an option. If an agreement is reached he pays the agreed option fee, sets about securing planning permission for 'change of use' and, if all falls into place, completes the deal.

Lease options

Lease options have become a popular strategy lately, where it enables people to get into property with little or no money. You may have heard in the various network meetings 'buy a house for a pound'. Well strictly speaking you're not, you are buying the 'option' to buy the house, for a pound, the price of the house will be determined and will be not far off the market rate, it's just that you don't have to buy it now. In fact the 'option' will state that you have the 'option' to buy the house, but not the 'obligation', meaning at the maturity date of the option, you can walk away or assign/transfer your option to another person in order to make the purchase.

To explain, I thought I would give you another real example.

Last year a relative recommended a friend who owned a house in my area to contact me, the circumstances were that the owners did not live in the locality, in fact they lived 300 miles away. The house had been left to them some years before, they had been renting it out but being a remote investor inevitably experienced the problems associated with what I call 'long arm landlords.' The local lettings agents weren't doing a good job, there were voids and, as the landlord was not local, he found running the house a pain in the backside, having to do a round trip of 600 miles to resolve problems.

The landlord had just released funds via a re-mortgage from the property to invest closer to home, so could not sell, I was asked if I could help. It occurred to me that the best option here was a 'lease option' we would agree a monthly fee for which I would effectively rent the house for a given period and at the end of that period I would pay the agreed amount. In the meantime I would take over the house as if it were mine; fully managed, there would be no recourse to the owner in the event of repairs or maintenance costs.

At this time I had been talking to my son Ben about getting him into property and this was an Ideal opportunity; as he was 19 and at college he was unable to get a mortgage, so I explained this deal to him and he accepted. I would act as guarantor for him with the vendor and the vendor was very happy to enable Ben to get his foot on the property ladder.

The deal was agreed for the option, this was that we would pay £350 per month and would conclude the option in 3 years with a payment of £86,000. The property had been valued by the vendor for £114,000 from which he has just released £83,000, don't ask me why he didn't ask for more, I guess he was looking at the most efficient way of moving forward, every month that the house was empty he was paying the council tax, he was funding the re-mortgage and whilst the house was empty he was at risk that it could be broken into. So reasonably 'motivated'.

In 3 years Ben would be 22 and in a position to secure a mortgage and confident that the valuation would enable him to pull the required £86,000 if not more. In order for us to cover the monthly payment of £350 per month a single let would only have brought us in approximately £475 per month, so, and I had pre planned this before I agreed to the option, we set about creating a 5 bedroom HMO. The house had a large separate lounge with a large dining room off the kitchen, a ground floor shower room inc WC and a separate WC in the hallway. Upstairs there were 2 double bedrooms, single bedroom and a large bathroom, which had a corner bath and a shower.

We fitted a fire door to the ground floor lounge proving fire protection to that room, fitted a fire door to the kitchen and fire doors to all the rooms upstairs, we stripped out the bathroom suite and changed the obscure glass to clear and made this another single bedroom. In addition we fitted an interlinked smoke detection system as required.

I provided the funds to do the works on the basis that when the HMO starts returning a profit that I will recover my investment. This HMO is in area where the clients would be either LHA or Blue Collar, hence the monthly rates.

The property has 4 tenants currently, the figures look like this.

Rental Income monthly.

Room 1	£260
Room 2	£280
Room 3	£280
Room 4	£240
Room 5	£0
Total	£1060

Outgoings

Council Tax	£105
Gas	£ 60
Electricity	£ 45
Water	£ 25
Option payment	£350
Insurance	£ 12
Total	£597

The house currently occupied at 80% is making a monthly profit of £463, when fully occupied there will be an additional £240, making a gross profit of £703 per month.

The cost of the conversion (the investment) was just under £3000, so the R.O.I (expressed as a percentage) would look like this.

Monthly profit x12 / Investment x 100

463x12= 5556/3000 = 1.85x100 = 185% at 80% occupancy, when full the ROI would be 281%.

Not bad for a first time property investment! Let's not forget the potential value of the property in 3 years' time. For example let's assume that the property goes up in value just 5%, it will value up at £119,700 but that is 'bricks and mortar.' As this is deemed as commercial property I will look to raise funds from a commercial lender and get 70% of the gross annual income multiplied by a factor 8.

Gross annual income £15,600 x 8 = £124,800 x 70% = £87,360

From this Ben will have to pay the option settlement of £86,000, once he has paid the legal fees and bank charges he won't have anything left in his pocket, but it won't have cost him anything either. His monthly repayment costs will rise to around £500 per month, so his net profit when the house is full will drop to £533 per month.

Have half a dozen of properties like this and that's over £3000 per month for little outlay.

CHAPTER 3

Dealing with Builders - How to get the best deals

Chapter 3.
Dealing with Builders - How to get the best deals

My relationship with builders has traditionally been one where I am in control of the project I prepare the schedule of work and generally determine the prices I am prepared to pay based on the going rates from my experience.

So, in order for you to get the best prices for any given project you need to arm yourself; knowledge is key.

For example, recently there was an improvement scheme undertaken in the streets where I own a couple of properties, the houses were being clad in external insulation and rendered as part of a thermal improvement scheme funded by one of the energy companies under the 'Green deal' scheme. In one particular house the boiler was deemed not to have been old enough to be replaced within the scheme, but it was failing. I called the plumber who was doing the replacement boilers as I had seen his van parked often in the street.

The phone call went like this:

Me: "Hi, is that Andrew"?

Plumber: "Er Yes, how can I help you"

Me: "My name is Mike Woods and I see you're doing the plumbing works for the green deal works in Mary St, I've got a few properties around there and I need a combi boiler replacing as it wasn't included in the scheme. What will you charge me to do a straight swap"?

Plumber: "Oh yes no problem, What is there at the moment and where is it'?

Me: It's a combi, wall-mounted in the kitchen, horizontal flue within 600mm of the outside wall, it'll be a straight replacement, probably a little messing about with the pipes as the original ones may not line up with the new connections, but I'm sure nothing that you couldn't deal with".

Plumber: 'Yeah, that's fine, well I'll do it for you the same price as I charge the main contractor £2000, that Ok"?

Me: "Er, no, not at all".

There was a silence that I left for a while.

Plumber: "Why, what are you looking to pay"

Me: "Well" I replied, "I understand that you are Gas Safe registered, but if were to pay you £150 for the day, and you wouldn't take a day, and the boiler wouldn't be more than £800, I can't see how you arrive at two grand; look, I'm not somebody who you can take for a ride. Do you want to do the job or not"?

Plumber: "Er, well, when do you want it doing"?

Me: "When you can, as soon as possible, and I will buy the boiler and get it there for you, when do you want it"?

Plumber: "Ok, As it happens I just had a job cancelled for Saturday morning, can you get the boiler there by then"?

Me: "Yes, no problem, so how much"?

Plumber: "Oh, er, it's going to have to be 200 quid to make it worth my while, and I'll give you a Gas Safety certificate, OK"?

Me: Ok I said, I'll have the boiler there Friday by 5pm, ready for you in the morning".

Plumber: "Ok, I'll let you know when it's done"

I went to my Plumbing supplier and bought a Ferrolli 28HC wall-mounted Condensing boiler and flue kit for £500 including VAT and delivered it to the house that Friday evening as agreed. I sent a text to my tenant in the morning and asked if the plumber was there, she replied that he had arrived at 9am.

I received a text from the plumber at 12.30, that simply said "Job done".

So, not bad for a mornings work- £200.

Mike's tip!

Get to know the daily rates for various tradesmen, learn what typical jobs should cost, to ensure you're not being over charged, this will save you £'s

What you need to do is get an understanding of how a builder arrives at providing you with a quotation for a given job. In order to get an accurate price you need to be as accurate as possible with your schedule of work. In addition when dealing with smaller builders and individuals try and find out what the going rate per day is. It's not difficult, you just need to ask. Often tradesmen will say, "I don't work on a day rate basis, I charge by the job", which is fair, as he will be trying to get all the work needed to be done for a lump sum price. So you need to learn what typical jobs cost.

Also, you need to select a builder that is appropriate for the type of work you want him to do.

There are a number of ways depending the size of the project to go about it.

The first is dealing with a Main contractor, by this I mean a building firm that will undertake projects over £40-50,000, more in some regions, these firms will have large overheads; vans, offices, secretaries all of these costs need to be covered. These costs are known in the trade as Overheads and Profit.

All contractors have them, but the bigger the firm the bigger the overheads. Typically, the contractor will price up a job and then add 20-25% for O/H and P then add the VAT.

Typically these firms will have a number of people on their books, tradesmen that specialise in building work, carpenters, plasterers, brick layers, electricians and plumbers. To keep these guys in full time employment will cost the firm a small fortune plus the firm will pay their taxes and national insurance payment. All of which will be passed on to you; you will get a thorough costing and a very good job done, but you will pay for it.

If you approach such a firm to do any smaller job than that they will probably decline to quote, because they know that they can't be competitive with the smaller guys.

The next way forward is to source a local builder from either Yell.com or by going to your local builders merchant and asking them to recommend someone, or indeed ask someone locally to recommend a firm if you're not based locally to the project. You may also, do a little tour of the area and look out for a Builders van parked outside a job, pull up and knock on the door and ask to speak to the boss, explain your circumstances and that you are looking for a reliable local builder. Hopefully he will be accommodating and show you around the job he's doing, if he's doing a good job he will be proud to show it off to you.

Mike's top tip!

Make sure you get a thorough understanding of how a builder arrives at providing you with a quotation for a given job. In order to get an accurate price you need to be as accurate as possible with your schedule of work. DO NOT make the mistake of skipping this important area as it can save you literally thousands of £'s in the long run!

Recommendations are really key in the building trade, so if you have found a builder ask him if he doesn't mind you going to see some of the other jobs similar to the one you want to have done and speak to former clients. Unfortunately builders have grown to have a bad reputation and some have been known to take advantage of the lack of knowledge of the lay person and massively over charge or simply charge for something that wasn't necessary.

We have all seen 'Cowboy Builders' on TV. But NOT all builders are rip off merchants, there are some thoroughly good guys out there who know their stuff and do a great job for the right money.

To me, it's the guys who don't know what they are doing who start to rip people off, because they don't assess the job properly, or there's the guys who do know and purposely under-estimate, then during the job they 'identify' to the client that something else needs to be done and then comes the hit, where it costs the clients disproportionately more; of course the client is committed and doesn't want the job to stop, so rolls over and agrees to the 'extra' work.

Again, you need to be as accurate as possible when asking for a quotation or tender.

Invite the builder to visit the property and be as firm and concise as possible; if you are vague about what you want, how can he put a firm price on it? Try and prepare a spreadsheet and if possible measure the rooms; measuring up takes time as does preparing quotes.

To be fair to the builders, the worst thing you can do early on is ask, "how much does he think the job will cost?" As a project manager, this question always comes. From my experience I will work out a ball park figure in my head, then add 10-20%. The problem when you tell a client a figure early on is this figure gets etched in stone in their heads, and without fail when the estimate or quotation is presented, you will hear, 'but you said it would be around £x'. So from experience I will endeavour to over-estimate to cover my backside.

I fully understand that as a relative new-comer to the world of property you can only rely on establishing trust with the tradesmen; using someone who has been recommended will be a good start.

In most small building firms you will have the boss - this guy has probably established his firm over the years from being good on the tools himself, either a bricklayer, plasterer or carpenter. As time has passed, no doubt customers have asked him to do jobs of varying complexity and he will have pulled in other tradesmen as and when he needs them, this is known as 'sub-contracting.' So he will have pulled together a team of tradesmen and will call on them as and when he needs them; by doing this he does not 'employ' them on a full time basis, they will pay their own taxes etc, therefore the builder's overheads are reduced. He may have one or two regular guys 'on the books' usually these will be very handy individuals who can turn their hand to many aspects of building works.

These 'multi taskers' are the type of guys I use, Whilst I agree 'no man can be a master of all trades', I have established contact with some really handy guys who can do carpentry work, masonry work, fit windows, basic electrics and plumbing, plastering and tiling. These are the type of guys I would recommend that you try to find, because you are dealing with just one or two builders, and if there is something that needs doing that needs the involvement of an electrician or gas engineer, he will no doubt know one and most importantly you will be charged the tradesmen' rates, not 'retail'. You will find when you eventually secure the services of a good builder and make sure you pay him on time and as agreed from the outset, he will look after your interests, even go out of his way to ensure you get materials and other services at the right prices.

Mike's tip!

Try and find a local Handy man, someone who can turn his hand to most building tasks, you will save hundreds of £'s in the long run.

If you want a basic refurbishment of a terraced or semi-detached house, prepare a list of work as follows:

A. Strip out existing bathroom suite, WC, bath and basin.
B. Remove existing wall tiles and prepare walls for new.
C. Install new 3 piece bathroom suite allow £300 for the supply
D. Fit new tiles to bathroom approx. 8m² tiles to be supplied by owner.
E. Strip out existing kitchen and existing wall tiles

F. Supply and fit new kitchen allow £2000 for kitchen.

A. Fit new tiles to kitchen approx. $4m^2$ tiles to be supplied by owner.

G. Redecorate whole house with 2 coats of magnolia emulsion to walls and 2 coats of white emulsion to ceilings. One coat of undercoat and White gloss to all woodwork.

H. Allow for 1 skip to remove debris from site

Or of course include any other items that are particular to the project, by doing this you are making life easier for the builder; remember that builders are good at building work, this is what they do in their day, it is in the evenings generally that they will go out to meet with new clients and visit a job enquiry. If you don't give them a list of work, they will need to prepare one themselves. They should also add amounts for unforeseen works, that from their experience they can expect; a 'contingency sum'.

If, of course when the job starts and they rip out the kitchen or bathroom and find that there has been a leak over the years and find some wet or dry rot that needs treating, then they will rightly bring this to your attention and advise you that there will be an additional cost, should you want them to do it while they are there.

If you select a builder that is VAT registered you will pay a little more, all building materials that go into a job will carry VAT at the standard rate of 20%, but if the builder is not VAT registered his labour cost will not carry VAT.

Example A. Non VAT Registered Builder

The above list of work is with a non VAT registered builder, the costing he will prepare would look something like this:

	Labour	Mats
A. Strip out existing bathroom	£200	
B. Remove existing wall tiles	£120	
C. Install bathroom suite	£250	£300
D. Fit new tiles to bathroom	£150	£140
E. Strip out kitchen and wall tiles	£240	

F. Supply and fit new kitchen	£600	£2000
G. Fit new tiles to kitchen	£80	£200
H. Redecorate whole house	£1000	£180
I. Allow for 1 skip		£180
Total		£3000
VAT on Materials		£ 600
Total	£2640	£3600

Total cost of works £6240

Example B. VAT Registered Builder

If the above list of work were with a VAT registered builder, the costing he will prepare would look something like this:

	Labour	Mats
A. Strip out existing bathroom	£200	
B. Remove existing wall tiles	£120	
C. Install bathroom suite	£250	£300
D. Fit new tiles to bathroom	£150	£140
E. Strip out kitchen and wall tiles	£240	
F. Supply and fit new kitchen	£600	£2000
G. Fit new tiles to kitchen	£80	£200
H. Redecorate whole house	£1000	£180
I. Allow for 1 skip		£180
Total	£2640	£3000
VAT	£ 528	£ 600
Total	£3168	£3600

Total cost of works £6768

As you can see from the above, by employing a non VAT registered builder it will save you £528 on the above list of works. In the event that there is more work required you would pay 20% more as you go along. And there should be no real difference in the quality of the work.

The rates that I have included are typical of what I would pay my tradesmen, that's not to say you will be able to get it done for the same, as it will depend on your region.

The next way forward is to consider a project manager, this type of thing is what I do for clients who want a project doing who do not live in the area.

I will meet with the clients, prepare a brief of the their requirements and then either give that schedule to a small crew of men, tradesmen that can either do the whole job by themselves, or the bulk of the work and I may call in an electrician or plumber to do the electrical work or any work to gas pipes etc, as needs be. I will get them to put costs against the works required and then once the total is reached I will add a 'management fee' of 10% or a minimum of £1500, as it's got to be worth my while arranging for the trades to do what they need and report to the clients.

Now as my project management company is VAT registered the example above will look like this:

	Labour	Mats
A. Strip out existing bathroom	£150	
B. Remove existing wall tiles	£100	
C. Install bathroom suite	£200	£220
D. Fit new tiles to bathroom	£120	£120
E. Strip out kitchen and wall tiles	£160	
F. Supply and fit new kitchen	£500	£1700
G. Fit new tiles to kitchen	£80	£160
H. Redecorate whole house	£900	£150
I. Allow for 1 skip		£180
Sub total	£2210	£2530
Project management 10%	£1500	
VAT	£1248	
Total	£7488	

Total cost of works £7152

Note that whilst I would charge VAT on all the costs the actual costs of the labour and materials will reduce because as project manager working regularly with tradesmen and suppliers I/they will be able to secure the labour and materials cheaper than what you would be able to. If you didn't live near the project and decided to run it yourself, you must ask yourself, how much is it costing you in time and fuel to go back and forth between home and the house over the duration of the project.

Your time is money, and it is false economy to try and do it all yourself. Recently I have met a few people who have invested in South Wales who do not live locally and in effort to save money, have undertaken some of the easier work like decoration themselves. I heard of a couple who were arriving mid-afternoon on a Friday, started to decorate, sleep on a makeshift bed, get up at the crack of dawn and paint all day and pack up early evening Sunday to return home. This job, which would take a decorator under 12-14 days, was taking over 5 weeks. You really must weigh up the fact that your property is either not being rented out or on the open market for sale during this period; either way you are potentially losing money. Not to mention the quality of the work going to be seen by your potential buyer or tenant.

Buying Materials and Dealing with Builders Merchants.

It amazes me to hear from some newbies that they have been buying materials for their refurbishment project from B&Q; whilst this DIY superstore can be of use, you really need to establish an account with a Builders merchants. As with all things in order to maximise your profits you must minimise your expenditure. Quite simply why pay £20 for an item when I can be purchased for £10.

In order to secure an account you will need to complete an application form and include the amount of monthly credit you require, usually £5,000. The merchants will credit check you and if all is well confirm your account. Once you have secured an account it is vitally important you meet with the branch manager and establish the likely materials that you will be buying on a regular basis. i.e. sand, cement, plaster, plasterboards, dry wall adhesive, screws, paint, etc.

Once you have done this you need discuss what is known as 'terms'

The merchant will have the 'retail' price of all their stock, so for example without an account, if you walked in off the street and bought 3 bags of cement and 15 small sacks of sand, they would charge you the retail price.

As an account holder the merchant will provide you with a discount rate across the list of items you intend buying; this discount will be applied to your account, so whenever you order something your terms will be applied to you invoice. As mentioned the merchant will apply a level of discount based on the volume of goods you may well intend to purchase. The amount of discount can vary between 30-60%.

It important that when you receive your invoices that you check what has been delivered. Often my crew will order something that is not a regular item and not on my terms list, the merchants back office will just apply the normal price to the invoice. On one occasion one of my guys ordered an extractor fan from the merchants as he needed it quickly. Now I usually buy my fans from Screwfix as they are cheaper there, so when I received my invoice from the merchants I called the branch manager about the price I had been charged, he altered my discount rate for all products from that particular manufacturer, and confirmed that I would get a 73% discount from then on! However, that item was still available cheaper in Screwfix. Once the merchant has agreed to the discount they will issue you with a credit note, which will appear on your end of month statement.

So, whilst you may have an account with a merchant you still need to be aware of other suppliers and the various prices they have. Often Screwfix and Selco will, if you register with them have monthly specials, where they may well have something priced attractively just when you need it.

I've been known to receive such a brochure in the post and gone and bought a dozen items knowing that at some time they will come in useful.

Another supplier that you should contact is Howdens for kitchens, doors and ironmongery, again you need to establish the terms of your account. There are other online suppliers that I use, which you don't need to have an account for and they still provide excellent prices and offer next day delivery.

As part of my 'How to Successfully Invest in Property' Master Class delegates who come on the training will be able to benefit from my association with one of the national Builders merchants and be able to take advantage of the same level of discount that I receive. Ultimately saving hundreds of pounds from their orders.

If you have gone to the trouble of establishing accounts with builders merchants and the like, when you approach a builder to do the work you can offer that you will supply the material and that you only need him for his labour. This is quite often very acceptable to the smaller guys, as they do not need to 'fund' the cost of the materials and there is less risk on their part as they are less financially exposed. What you will need to do is give him your account details at the merchant and have him 'call off' what is needed. It is advisable that you contact the branch and notify them, giving them authority to receive orders from your appointed builder. Of course the more paranoid of you will be worried that the builder may over order and use your materials on another job. Your concerns may be well founded, so, as mentioned it comes down to establishing a relationship and trust. Just ensure that the builder adds a reference to the invoice to ensure you know what he has ordered.

If the project is close to your home, you can have a daily input on site, see what materials are on site and how the job is progressing. If the project is remote to you, you can establish with the builder that he notifies you of what he has ordered as and when and then you can track the materials when you receive the invoice. The merchants will issue the invoices within a day or so of the delivery or collection, so it not like you won't know what's been ordered until the end of the month.

At the end of the month you will receive a statement from the merchant listing your purchases and you will then have a further 30 days to pay.

By doing things this way you have greater control of the cost of the materials as when the contractor supplies materials he will not charge you the same as what he has been charged; he may in fact 'mark up' the material that he has supplied. After all why should you fully benefit from the discounts he has built up over the years by being a good customer of the merchant?

Mike's top tip!

Set up an account at your local builders merchants, Also register with other suppliers and subscribe to their monthly offer newsletters. Use these deals to drive costs down.

The Italian Job.

I thought I would share this story with you as not only is it is relevant to this section, but also gives you an insight into the mind set of being a property investor and entrepreneur.

In late 2005, my wife Syvona was looking into where we could go for our future summer holidays, Maddison was one year old, and Syvona didn't want to be stuck at home trying to find things to entertain Maddi for the future summers. I'm sure those of you that are parents, will agree that it is not cheap entertaining children or going on day trips in the UK in the summer holidays.

She had looked on-line at renting a villa in the South of Italy for the summer holidays and once she had found a few places brought them to my attention, she had been looking at places large enough to accommodate not only us, but my mother and her brother's family.

The places she showed me looked lovely, but when I saw the prices! These villas large enough for 6 to 8 people were £2000 per week, so for 6 weeks that was going to be cool £12,000. 'You must be joking' I said, 'I can buy one for that'. Knowing me as she does, she said, 'Why don't we then' and set off with all the reasons she could muster to persuade me it would be great in the long term.

I must admit I did like the idea of owning a place abroad, I have always enjoyed watching 'A place in the Sun' particularly when Italian places were featured. I had seen a few programs on Tuscany and having got married there had some affection toward Italy.

So, I set about doing some research; it was apparent to me that the smaller properties without swimming pools were not as popular as the larger properties with swimming pools, and the rates being charged whilst they were listed for the rental of the property per week, there was some correlation between the prices and the number of people it could sleep.

I had gathered that most places were being booked up from June to mid September, so a rental period of 15 weeks at £2000 would return £30,000, of course if we were to be there for 6 weeks the net income would be around £18,000 if fully let.

So the next task was to see what a place in Puglia would cost. If you follow me on Facebook or check out our website at www.trullowithpool.co.uk you will see that the traditional houses in that region are called Trulli. These are stone buildings with conical shaped roofs, some are many are hundreds of years old. These were the buildings that were being booked up more that the modern villas. I searched on various web sites by typing all variations of the words trullo for sale. I came up with a number of agents and my research showed that Puglia, whilst still off the main tourist map, was becoming more popular since Ryanair had started routes into Brindisi and Bari Airports, both within an hour of the area I was focusing on which was called the Valle d'Itria and the towns of Martina Franca and Ceglie Messapica.

It has never interested me in buying into a complex of flats or apartments of the like of Spain, my philosophy has always been to buy something that has something different about it, something unique that would be easy to sell on one day.

I found that there were numerous properties for sale ranging from £50,000 to £300,000, I had set a budget of £100,000, which was available between bank accounts and equity in the rental properties.

So, in January 2006 Syvona and I were on a plane bound for Puglia; I had emailed several agents with my requirement and lined up viewing over a three day period. We were in for a shock; it was apparent that the Italian and British agents were not good at updating their websites so many of the properties that were advertised, were either no longer available, probably never available even, just show cases. We were taken to various properties, which were completely wide of the mark of what we were looking for and in the wrong location and in some cases completely uninhabitable.

Mike's tip!

When considering buying something abroad it is essential to buy something that has something different about it, something unique that would make it more attractive to let and sell on one day.

But two places caught our eye, both completely different. The first was a villa close to the sea, it was basically a shell that either we could finish off or employ the builder to complete, it had a lovely flat roof terrace with sea views and was within the budget to buy and I would need to find some more money to complete it. The second property was a trullo and a villa, In Puglia each trullo cone forms a room and this trullo had 8 cones compared to most that we had seen which had 4 or 5.

The property was vacant and had not been lived in for some years; it needed thoroughly updating especially if we were going to attract rental figures of £2000 per week. The property was set back of the main road, it had iron gates and a 100m long stone driveway, and it needed to have a swimming pool. At the time the exchange rate between the Pound and the Euro was 1.45 so my budget was €145,000, and this place was on at €130,000, but I would need to find more money to renovate it and build the pool.

Syvona and I headed toward the airport and stopped for some dinner in a small town and discussed the two properties; whilst the villa was new and close to the beach it was not in the centre of the Valle d'Itria and there was just something special about the trullo, it was unique, different to anything else we had seen and it was positioned on the South side of a hill and had fabulous views over the surrounding country side. Although we didn't admit it to each other immediately, we both knew we wanted to buy it. But I was going to have to sort out the money.

Once home we contacted the agent and made an offer and chipped another €10,000 off the price, which was accepted by the family selling the property.

Whilst I was looking to purchase the property with my own funds, being able to get a mortgage on it would be ideal, as I would be able to fund the whole thing with money I had, so I set about searching the internet for an International Mortgage specialist. I found a guy who was based in London who was able to source mortgages in Italy. The first company he found was called Banco Woolwich, no surprises who they were, and as it happened my house in the UK is with the Woolwich, which is the private lending arm of Barclays.

Unfortunately when they were presented with my financial documents proving my affordability, they deemed that I was a developer and that this product was strictly domestic, so they declined to lend. Then the broker found an Italian bank called Uni Credit Banca who would provide a mortgage. The products available were a lifetime fixed rate (20yrs) or a standard variable repayment mortgage again over 20 years. I didn't like the idea of being locked into a fixed rate for 20 years so opted for the variable rate product. Both mortgages were 70% ltv.

Again, in retrospect this was a good move for, as in the UK, the interest rate in the EU has tumbled and so has my Italian Mortgage.

As in the UK I paid a survey fee and the bank instructed a surveyor and he agreed the valuation based on the agreed purchase price. So, happy days! I was in receipt of a mortgage offer and was away. I needed to pay a deposit of 30% and I could use the rest of the money for the refurbishment. Perfect!.

The property was purchased at the end of March and Syvona and I arranged to go over for Easter sign to the papers and have a week's holiday there with Maddi and Ben. We rented a small villa from and English couple who had been living in Puglia for a few years. As it happened they had recently had a pool built by a local specialist, I had a good look around it and asked if they could arrange for me to meet the chap.

The next day I met with pool guy- Piero at the trullo and explained the best I could what I wanted, Architectural drawings being the ultimate in communications my requirements were understood. In order to undertake the work I needed to appoint a Geometra (surveyor) to prepare the Planning application and submit them to the local council for approval. Of course he knew someone, who was working in the local council, so getting it approved was not going to be an issue.

This couple also recommended a builder that they had used and contacted him for me, following which we met at the trullo.

Whilst at the trullo I surveyed the building and the grounds and once I returned to the UK, prepared plans of my proposals and emailed them to the Geometra and to Piero, Piero was totally professional and prepared a detailed quotation, a Preventivo, which included everything I needed, even a computer that chemically converts salt into chlorine, so the pool water cleans itself when I'm not there, not a cheap bit of kit, but I needed it.

So, I needed to find someone I could rely on to help me during the project, so I searched online and found a forum that had set up by English people living in Puglia, I joined up and started to ask questions etc and found two people who I came to rely on, one was an English guy who was a plumber and the other an Italian, Diego, who was a Geometra in another town. He was starting up an estate agency and I found him to be very trustworthy.

I arranged a visit back to Puglia alone and started to pull the project together. It dawned on me that other than the plumber and Diego, not many people spoke English in the middle of Southern Italy; in order to get a handle on things fully I needed to learn how to speak Italian. I searched online again, and found a CD box set by a chap called Michel Thomas, he taught other languages but his style was unique, he taught it as one would speak it, he didn't concentrate initially on past, present and future tenses, so I plugged in my head phones at night and played the CDs in the car or where-ever I went.

Once I had returned to Martina Franca, I met with the builder and went through what was needed, I arranged to meet the plumber and Diego at the house and took them through my requirement. I asked Diego if he would be my eyes and ears whilst I was not there; he was to make regular visits and send me emails with photos of the work and updates.

In addition to the builder, the agent that I had purchased the trullo from had asked if his builder could tender for the work, which I agreed to, so I gave both builders a list of work which Diego translated for me and awaited the costs.

The quotation received from Piero, the pool builder at €26,000 was acceptable and he had included for a non-slip marble paving to be laid around the pool, but when I received the quotes from the builders I was staggered. I had worked out the costs based on what I would expect to pay in the UK, now it wasn't like the building industry in Puglia was booming, Italy was experiencing the same decline as the rest of Europe, building materials were not more expensive, I had sussed that out, they were taking the Mick! Word had it that many British people 'with money' were retiring in the South and the builders saw this as rich pickings, well sorry, not me. The quote from the Italian builder was €75,000 not including tiles, bathroom suites and paving of which there was 250m² and the quote from the English agent was €105,000 but did include some materials. These quotes were ridiculous, just because I didn't understand the language didn't mean I was stupid.

I returned to the UK and ripped the costing apart, I was convinced that I could get this work done for around €60,000 including the materials. The pool, the central heating and domestic water supply were going to be in addition. I decided that I would have to sub contract the work and run it myself and besides, it would be an adventure.

I agreed the contract with the plumber which was €20,000 who introduced me to an electrician whose quote I had agreed to, and instructed them to make a start.

So, in October 2006, I booked flights with Ryanair from Stansted to Brindisi every 3 weeks starting in January through to April, choosing mid-week flights, Ryanair at the time had deals on where you could fly for £1 depending on the quiet slots. I ended up paying £35 for return flights. It was costing me more in fuel driving from South Wales to Stansted than flying to Italy.

During my visits to the trullo I would stay in a B&B in the small town of Ceglie Messapica called Villa Kailia, there the couple who ran it were typical welcoming Italians and I asked the husband if he knew where I could get new windows and doors made; the original ones at the trullo were wooden and single glazed, they needed to be renewed. He offered to take me to see his friend who made windows and doors in aluminium, perfect, just what I wanted, and of course in Italy his friend is my friend, so I had the windows and doors at the right prices, for what I expected pay. I then asked if he knew where I could buy bathroom fittings and tiles, the next thing I knew I was in the car going to see a brilliant young man called Damiano, I told him I was an Architect in the UK, I had bought a trullo and wanted 3 bathroom suites, floor tiles and wall tiles. He couldn't have been more helpful and he offered me 'terms' of 55% discount.

I had sourced a kitchen supplier and agreed a price for the supply and fitting of the units including fridge/freezer, washing machine and dishwasher, but no work tops as I wanted marble and the plumber had taken me to a specialist. Marble work tops in Italy are cheaper than formica worktops. And I got them supplied and fitted for a few hundred Euros.

Things were coming together nicely, all I needed now was a good general builders, through the forum I came across a guy whose name I will not mention, he specialised in wall building, he didn't do it himself but fronted for a small crew of Albanian wall builders. In Puglia the boundary walls around properties and those that define boundaries in fields are all done by hand, dry stone walls using locally quarried stone. I wanted the perimeter of the pool to have a wall 900mm high to protect the area from the breeze and I wanted the pool area set down 450mm (3 steps) from the main piazalle (patio) and a wall between that we could plant flowers in to break up the areas.

I arranged to meet this chap during a visit and he showed me the different quality of dry stone walls his team could build, I agreed the quality and agreed the deal. I wanted 100m of wall and it was €60 per metre material and labour included.

Piero the pool specialist had made a start on excavating the pool and I marked out where I wanted the walls to be built and left them to it.

Speaking to this chap, I told him that I needed a general builder to do the remaining works and he brought someone along. What we agreed was that I prepare a list of work and how much I was prepared to pay for each task and he would let me know if it was acceptable, after a little light hearted banter and typical hand gesturing we agreed a price.

I returned to the UK and left them all to get on, I was sent regular updates by the various guys and all seemed to be progressing well. I returned a few week later and was not happy with the quality of the dry stone walls around the pool. It wasn't what I had expected when looking close up. From the photos it looked OK, but standing in front of it, I wasn't happy, they had completed about 70% of the walls and I had paid instalments of €4500 to the manager.

I knew that I would not be satisfied in the years to come floating in the pool; I would hate those walls. The workmen were not there when I arrived and I summoned their manager to come to the property. He arrived sometime later and I expressed my dissatisfaction, pulling the loose small stones out of the wall that were not tied in properly. Ok, Ok he said I will get them to put it right, they did not return during that visit and he said that they would be there on the following Tuesday, I told him in no uncertain terms that I did not want them to do any more, but rectify what they had done. I would return to the UK on my scheduled flight and then come back on the next available flight, 3 days later and we would go from there.

I arrived at the house on the Tuesday only to find that they had completed all the walls, I was furious, and it was not better than I had last seen it. I called the guy on the phone and told him I wanted to see him and the wall builders as soon as possible. Around 4pm they all turned up, the manager and 4 Albanians. I showed them what I was not happy with and argued that this quality was not what I had agreed to, and that I wanted it to be re-done, at which point the manager, put up his hands and said 'I'm only the interpreter', got in his car and drove off.

The Albanian wall builders, just stood there and then said 'Soldi' to me which means 'money' or 'payment', I just laughed at the guy, he couldn't speak any English and my Albanian wasn't any better. I shook my head and said 'No', the general builder was present so I called him over and asked him to explain that I had paid their manager €4500 and that I wasn't paying any more.

They told my builder that they had received only €1800 and wanted the rest of their money. I refused point blank and told them 'where to go', not sure if they understood this 'different language', but after an hour they got the message and got in their car and drove off.

I spoke to my general builder and he reinforced my view that this work was not acceptable, and he took me to see some dry stone walls his Albanian wall builders had done and it was beautiful. If you look at my website you will see the walls, whilst its not normal to comment in such a way about walls, but you will see what I mean when you know that these walls are built by hand and from boulder stone then split and chiselled to shape.

The stone can also vary from quarry to quarry, the Cream colour stone is far better quality that the White stone available.

I instructed the builder to demolish all the walls that had been built and take the stone away, I wanted new walls in the better stone laid in the proper manner. He agreed the rate of €60 per metre for the labour and materials, and I had to write off €4500, lesson learned.

Three weeks later I was back at the trullo, work was progressing well, the pool was taking shape, the electrician had finished, the plumber was nearly done and the bathrooms were taking shape, all the bathroom suites and tiles had been delivered and fitted, the windows had been installed and most of all I was there or thereabout on course for my budget of €60,000 (not including the €4500 hit on the walls).

The guys would start work around 6.30am and finish around 1pm as it was now June and the weather was getting hotter. One afternoon all the guys had gone and I was in the trullo on my own fitting some wall lights and heard a car coming down the drive, I wasn't expecting anyone, I looked out of the window and could see it was the first Albanian wall builders, they must have heard I was back or seen me in the town.

So, I wondered how I was going to handle this, the doors were wide open my car was there and to be honest I wasn't going to hide from them, so by the time they got out of their car I had travelled the 20 metres or so and was standing ready for them. "What do you want" I said, not that they could understand me, but I motioned hand open in front of me, again as before, they said "soldi", I repeated myself, by now I had become reasonably well spoken in Italian, and told them I had paid what I was going to and no more, their walls had been removed and had been replaced by far superior work.

They said that they had no money for food and that they had not been paid any more by their manager; he had told them that he had not received the amount I had paid him, and they wanted their money from me. They motioned that they would knock down the walls built by my new guys, to which I told them they would be sorry. This stand-off lasted another hour, eventually they could see that they were not getting anywhere with me and reluctantly drove off.

After they had gone I called my builder and told him of the altercation, he asked me if I was OK and asked me to go over to his town to meet him for dinner. Over dinner and a beer I explained a little more about the events in particular the threats they made about knocking down the walls. Vito made a call to his wall builder, typically Italian, even between friends there were raised voices. Vito hung up and said, "we wait'. An hour later his phone rang, he just nodded and agreed with the caller. He hung up and simply said. "Niente piu" which means 'no more'.

Obviously, my wall builder had contacted the other guys and warned them off from coming round again.

The work continued and in the August of 2007 we turned up for our first summer holiday at our newly named Trullo Monte d'oro.

We were all done for under €120,000, Building work, materials, Central heating, hot and cold water throughout and the Pool, I was very pleased with myself, I must say.

If you go the website as mentioned you will see under the rattan pergola a wooden dining table, it is there that I am sitting writing this very section, and at this point I am going to have a break and jump in the pool as its 33 degrees.

We have spent many weeks a year at the trullo and have become very good friends with our neighbours Pietro and Margarita, they are both in their early seventies and a typical Southern Italian family, they are completely self-sufficient they grow and rear everything they eat. Pietro rears two pigs every year for pork, he has rabbits and chickens. Their garden is full of fresh vegetables and he has a vineyard and olive grove. They never stop working the land, whenever I go over to see them they are always doing something, splitting Almonds, stuffing figs or Margarita is making fresh pasta. I really respect them, they don't have much by way of money, but they are always smiling and give us a really warm welcome.

I will call them on the phone a day or two before we go over as they hold the keys of the house for us, they will ask what time we are arriving and if we arrive around lunch time or dinner time they will have prepared the table for us, they are wonderful people.

Since being there which is now over seven years, we have become friendly with their friends and Pietro will often come over in the day and say that we must be at their house at 7pm because we are going to visit their friends for dinner and we are invited, you just can't put a price on that hospitality.

Of course Maddison has made friends with another little girl her own age and we will take them both to the beach as her parents work throughout the summer and she stays with her nana, so to have the day out with us at the beach, the fun fair or to come to our house and play in the pool all day is great fun for them both.

So all in all buying a house in Italy has been one of the best decisions I have made, 'it washes its own face' which means the money that it earns is more than it costs per year and effectively provides us with a free holiday home.

In addition it is now valued at more than double what it cost me to buy and refurbish.

From 2015 I will be inviting my clients to the trullo for 2 or 3 day Mind Set and coaching sessions and in the evenings taking clients out to dinner in the local town, but one night will be at Pietro and Margarita' house eating fresh home-made pasta, home-made sauces and drinking Pietro's Red wine. Bellissima!

CHAPTER 4

Building Regulations and Planning

Chapter 4. Building Regulations and Planning

The Building Regulations.

What are they and how do they affect you? The Building Regulations are a set of Documents approved and issued in the UK by the Secretary of State for the purpose of providing practical guidance for some of the more common building situations. They set minimum standards for the design and construction of all buildings and require that any work should be carried out with proper materials and in a good workmanlike manner and they are made for specific purposes, these being Health and Safety, energy conservation and the welfare and convenience of disabled people.

The regulations are set out in a series of 'manuals' known as 'Parts' and are there to ensure that national standards of building work are being undertaken whether it be a small house extension, a new house, a new factory, office or your house renovation.

The regulations are administered by your local Authority Building Control Section and you are required to make an application (and pay a fee) if the work you propose to undertake falls within what is known as 'relevant works' or you are making a 'material change' to the building.

For most light refurbishments or renovation works where you are replacing a bathroom, kitchen and perhaps inserting a DPC it is not necessary to submit an application, however where people fall foul is that the Approved Document Part L (which relates to Conservation of Fuel and Power) applies should you hack off the external render or internal plaster of an external wall.

The update to that 'Part' which was in 2006 requires that as you are 'replacing or renovating a thermal element in a building' i.e. a wall, then you have the opportunity to improve the insulation value of that wall by adding either External or Internal wall insulation.

Now that you have fallen into the realms of the Building control section as you are undertaking 'relevant works or making a material change' they will be interested to know what 'other' work you are undertaking to ensure that it meets the required standards.

Now in all honesty this is nothing to be concerned about providing you are doing the work properly and in good workmanlike manner, after all should your refurbishment project be such that you intend to sell on, your purchasers surveyor will pick up upon the fact that you may have done 'relevant works' or made a 'material change' and may stipulate to the lender that you provide the necessary Building Regulations Completion Certificate.

Mike's tip!

If you're not sure if the work you are undertaking falls under the Building Regulations, Call your local Office. Making an application retrospectively can be costly adding unnecessary costs and stress to your project.

So, what sections of the Building Regs do you need to be aware of to ensure that you stay within the law and avoid your project going over budget?

The main Parts that affect Renovations and Refurbishments are:

Part A –Structure

This Part deals with structural stability of the building and covers foundations, floors, walls (internal and external) and roofs.

For example:

Foundations: If you are looking to knock down a wall and install a steel beam, you may find that an internal wall remaining that you intend 'bearing' on is not strong enough to carry the additional 'point' load. Think of it like the a woman' shoe, the sole part of the shoe can spread the load, whereas the stiletto is concentrating the load. If the stiletto is too slender it will collapse or punch through (subside). So, it may be necessary to build a small pier or column in blockwork, this will have to sit and be built off a small concrete foundation, usually 600x600x225mm, and will need to be dug into the original ground.

Floors: If you are replacing an old timber floor with a new solid concrete floor, this construction must include a sub base (hardcore) and DPM, Insulation and the concrete slab itself. Some people will lay a sand cement screed (50mm) over the slab to get a level finish. The insulation to be installed will be guided by the BCO, the requirement for the thickness in a new build is determined by other factors, so in a refurb any amount of insulation is better that what was there before i.e. nothing. Its normal to add at least 50mm of a polystyrene insulation. This insulation can be placed either above or below the DPM. The concrete floor must also be of a suitable mix and the sub base must be at least 150mm thick and compacted.

Internal walls: If you intend removing a wall to make a room larger and the wall is load bearing, meaning it is carrying either the floor above or a solid wall above, then you will need to insert a beam or RSJ (rolled steel joist) to be able to 'carry' the load from above. For this you will need to submit an application and provide calculations from a structural engineer to prove that the beam is adequate to carry the imposed loads. However I have found that from my experience and that of the Building Inspector that we can agree on site that a particular RSJ size would be satisfactory to do the job, so by all means ask your Inspector if he is able to advise you of an acceptable size of beam, before you go spending £250 on structural calculations.

In addition there are companies such as Catnic and IG Lintels who supply fabricated beams and are catalogued as being suitable for internal openings both load bearing and non-load bearing, light duty and heavy duty and are sold based on the loading and length. So, for example if you are opening up a room and the span of the opening is 3m, you may find that a 'light duty' beam may only go up to 2.4m, therefore you need to choose a 'heavy duty beam'. These companies will provide a technical service where they can advise in 'typical domestic' situations which beam will suit the particular requirements.

Roofs: Often older properties have slate roofs and over time these have sagged, this is where the original rafters and supporting timbers i.e. purlins were undersized when originally built (before building regs). If this is the case you would be advised to improve the construction by adding some additional supporting timbers. A common mistake people make when replacing a slate roof is to refit interlocking concrete tiles. What people don't realize is that these tiles are 30% heavier than the original slate. So strengthening the roof structure is highly recommended.

In addition, it is common in roof timbers to find them to be rotten and decayed, this is due primarily to leaks and condensation. When re-roofing it is recommended that you address any leaks, and advisable to renew any timbers with like sizes and you will need to either add ventilation to the loft or use a breathable membrane.

Part B- Fire

This Part deals with installing systems that provide 'early warning' of fire, ensuring that there is a safe route to the outside and to stop the spread of fire.

Usually unless you are redesigning the layout of the house and making it open plan, where the stair is not in a protected route to the outside, the requirement would be for you to install an interlinked smoke detection system instead of the battery operated ones.

Also in this event of creating an open plan living area including a stair in the room, you will then need to look at the opening arrangement of the first floor bedroom windows, these will need to be 'escapable' in the event of a fire.

Part F- Ventilation

This Part deals with ventilation to prevent the build-up of condensation in roof voids and within the dwelling, which will lead to damp problems. (See section in Defects)

In the event that you are creating a new en-suite or utility room then you will need to install an appropriately sized extractor fan.

Part H- Drainage and Waste disposal.

This Part deals with the removal of waste water and rain water. In the event of you installing the aforementioned en-suite or utility room then you are required to ensure that the waste water from toilets, basins and sinks are collected through the correctly sized pipes and discharged into the foul drainage system.

For example, a Toilet must connect to a soil pipe with a minimum diameter of 100mm, a kitchen sink, bath or shower must be 38mm diameter and a basin or sink 32mm diameter. This section also requires that each drainage facility must be fitted with 'traps'.

Part K- Protection from falling, Collision and Impact.

This Part deals with staircases, balustrading and guarding to balconies. So if you install a totally new staircase, say to provide access to an attic room in the house, the stair, balustrading and handrail design and layout of the items will need to comply with the requirements, these involve maximum tread heights known as 'risers' and minimum tread width- known as 'goings', also there are minimum height of handrails and balustrading.

If you are simply replacing a staircase with like for like, then this is not a 'material change' or if you change the arrangement slightly but not make the situation any worse than it was originally, the same applies.

Part L- Conservation of Fuel and Power.

This part deals with standards required to ensure maximum energy efficiency to all parts of the building including wall insulation, floor insulation, loft insulation, pipework insulation and windows.

This Part has traditionally been one of the main ones referred to in the design of new dwelling and buildings; however, in 2006 the document was amended and includes 'Renovation' in relation to Thermal Elements, which means 'the provision of a new layer in the thermal element or the replacement of an existing layer', as mentioned previously this requires you to improve the heat loss efficiency of existing walls in the event that the Internal plaster or external render is being replaced.

For example: If you hack off the internal plaster or external render, you are deemed to be making a material change to the wall and therefore must improve its thermal efficiency, there are two ways to do this, either insulate the wall internally by adding at least 50mm of insulation to the inner face of the wall and then finishing with plasterboard or by adding 90-100mm of polystyrene insulation batts to the outside face of the wall and rendering over. You may well have seen local authority houses or a number of terraced houses having this work done under the 'Green deals' funded by the energy companies.

Part M- Access to and the Use of Buildings.

This Part deals with making living in a house easier for people with disabilities. In the event that you are undertaking a replacement electrical system in the house, you will be required to set the switches at certain heights. If you introduce a WC on the ground floor there must be sufficient space to allow wheel chair access. You are also not permitted to remove a WC on the entrance level of a house unless you propose to replace it elsewhere on that level, and that facility must not be less compliant than the original.

Part P- Electrical Safety.

This Part applies to the Design and Installation of electrical work to ensure that the work has been undertaken by a competent person. So, if you intend on replacing any electrical cables, change the consumer unit or adding equipotential (earth) bonding this Part applies to you.

If you are adding a new WC or Utility room as mentioned above you will need to install an extractor fan and hence new wiring.

So, there you have it. I would guess that some of you will be surprised that carrying out some of the work mentioned above will require you to submit an application to the Local Authority Building Control Section for their approval.

If you consider that you will need to submit an application, this is how you go about it.

You can either call your local offices and request an application form or go online and download one from your local Authority. However there are 2 ways to go about it.

The first Is where you submit a 'Full Plans' application, this would be used in the event that that your renovation works are substantial and you have gone to the length of employing someone to prepare plans i.e. An Architectural Technologist or even an Architect. Then you would submit the plans along with a fee for the plans to be 'vetted' and approved with conditions.

Following receipt of the approval, and once the works have commenced you will be sent an invoice from the BCO (Building Control Officer) for 'site inspections', which you must pay.

In the event that the works are not such that you need to have plans prepared, you can submit a 'Building Notice' the cost of which is the same as a Full Plans application and the Site Inspection fee together. plus VAT. Following your submission you are required to notify the BCO when you commence the work and he or she will arrange to visit you at the work to go through what is being done. The BCO will make arrangements for you to notify them as the works progress so that they can make regular inspections.

The fee that the BCO will charge is based on the 'value of the work'. This is where people can make a mistake and just pay what they are told. The best way for me to explain this is by example.

Say you are undertaking a refurbishment or renovation and the contractor you have employed has provided you with a quotation for £15,000. On the application form where it asks, 'estimated cost of work' you would be inclined to insert £15,000. The Building Control office have no clue at that point of the extent of the work so will accept your figure. The fee you pay is based on a scale relevant to the cost of the work.

However, there are large elements to the £15,000 that are not 'Relevant works' meaning that some of the work to be undertaken in the project does not need to comply with the Approved Documents, for example kitchen units, utility room units, tiling, doors etc.

In effect the work that you are undertaking to which the BCO is interested in may only equate to £5,000, therefore the fee applicable will be lower.

So, before you make your application, look closely at your costs and include only the cost of the work that relate to the Parts listed above.

Mike's top tip!

Always state at the application stage that you wish to receive a Completion Certificate on completion of the works, this will be required by your buyer's solicitor.

Building Regulations services are offered by Approved Independent Inspectors or practices, however, they still need to serve a notice to the Local Authority that they are administering the Building Control Services to you. I have used Independent Building control services in the past, but tend only to use them on new builds.

Planning Applications

If you are relatively new to property investing I would for the time being look to purchase property that needs light refurbishment. As you get more experienced you may feel more confident to progress to full refurbishments. I would avoid looking at property that is need of extensions, again until you are more proficient.

In the event that you do progress and do need or wish to extend a house or convert the garage to living accommodation you may well need to submit a Planning Application to the local authority. A Planning application consists generally of the following:

1. The planning application itself which provides details of you the applicant, the location of the work and the description of the work. You will need to confirm if you are the owner of the land and that it does not form part of an agricultural holding.
2. The application will require you pay a fee, which will be available from your LPA
3. The application will require you to submit scaled plans showing the existing elevations, plans and the proposed elevations and plans. You will need to show a block plan of the house in the context of the street.
4. An Ordnance Survey plan at a min scale of 1:1250 showing the location of the house.

The application forms and notes to assist you are available from your local planning department or you can make your application digitally via the on-line Planning Portal.

Whilst some of you may feel that you can put the plans together I would recommend that you employ someone who specialises in this. Most people automatically think they need an Architect, but there is an army of equally capable and talented people who are known as Architectural Technologists or Architectural Services; this is the banner under which I trade. By all means Google Architects and Architectural Services in your area and make some calls. The body that the Architectural Services firms are regulated by is called the Chartered Institute of Architectural Technologists (C.I.A.T.).

Try to avoid someone who you may be introduced to doing you a cash job; they are flying below the radar and will not have any insurances should something go wrong, and in the event you will probably find it difficult to get hold of them as they will probably be 'in work' in the day time. They will probably only give you their mobile number.

If someone calls me and asks me for a quote over the phone, I will ask detailed questions about the type of house, terraced or a semi etc, if you want a single or two storey extension, which way the roof will join into the existing house or existing roof. I have done so many of these over the years I am quite happy to give a ball park figure. If the people you ring aren't able to do that for you and start dragging the costs out, find someone else.

The Architectural guys should advise you if what you are proposing falls within the guidelines set by the Planning department. Whilst you may feel that the property is yours and you can do what you want, unfortunately that is not the case. Your extension must fall within the guidelines set, these are there to ensure that the proposals do not make the pattern of the existing development unsightly, (they will use the word 'incongruent') also your extension must not over-bear your neighbour's property or restrict light to habitable rooms.

Mike's tip!

By using an 'Architectural Services' firm as opposed a Architects firm can save you hundreds of £'s

The people that you appoint will need to visit the property and undertake a dimensional survey in order to prepare the existing plans and elevation, they will note the positions of drains and any in-coming gas, electrical or water services. They will prepare these plans and then produce the proposed plans and elevations, together with the block plan. This plan is usually to a scale of 1:200; it will show the outline of the house in the context of the adjacent properties, to show the planning officer the relationship of the proposed extension to adjacent houses.

As mentioned above your application can be submitted using the forms and drawing printed on paper or on-line. The professionals you employ should handle all this for you and will request that you either provide them with the application fee to forward on your behalf or request that you forward it directly.

A Planning application fee for an extension or a garage conversion, is classed as a 'home owner' application and the fee will be in the order of £165-180.

If you wish to convert an attic to habitable accommodation and install roof lights, normally unless you are in a conservation area a planning application is not required, this is called 'permitted development'.

If you are considering converting an attached garage, you will need permission, albeit nobody has probably ever parked a car in there because it was too small. The existing house will have a parking allocation, usually 2 off road spaces, by losing the garage you are changing the parking arrangements and the highways authority won't want to see the streets overcrowded with parked cars. If you can demonstrate that by widening the driveway to accommodate 2 cars side by side, this will usually be acceptable.

You will still need to submit an application to get the approval. You will also have to apply to the highways department to get the pavement crossover widened, most Highway authorities will not permit anyone to work on the adopted high way; you will therefore have to pay them to come out and undertake the work.

Permitted Development

Each local authority will have published guidelines for typical extensions which are available to you. Some small extensions are deemed to be 'permitted development' which means that you are allowed to undertake the work providing it falls within the approved guidelines. The guidelines vary from authority to authority however there has been some loosening of the planning laws in recent years, so by all means contact the LPA and request details of the extensions that are permitted. They are usually, rear single story that do not exceed 4 metre's high and do not project more than 4 metres from the rear of the main wall.

If your proposals do fall within the permitted development, I would take photographs before and after and apply to the LPA once the work is complete for a 'Certificate of Lawful development'. This is an essential piece of paper that will be needed whenever you wish to sell the property. The LPA will charge you a fee of around £50.

'Pieces of paper', that is certificates of conformity, are essential to ensure a smooth sales transaction, I can't stress this enough. Building Regulations Completion Certificates, Certificates of Lawful Use, FENSA Certificate and DPC and Timber treatment guarantees are the main ones.

This is because, when a valuation surveyor visits your newly refurbished house, he will note the fact that you have made improvements and will state on the valuation report that the solicitor is to obtain the relevant certificates and report to the lender prior to the lender releasing the funds; without them you won't get the funds.

Mike's tip!

If you do work to a property that is within the permitted development rights get a certificate of lawful use, this will save you a huge headache when you come to sell.

FENSA Certificates.

FENSA stands for the Fenestration Self-Assessment Scheme. Following Government encouragement, FENSA was set up by the Glass and Glazing Federation (GGF) and other industry bodies in response to Building Regulations for double glazing companies in England and Wales.

When replacing windows, doors and roof lights in dwellings in England and Wales, homeowners must comply with current thermal performance and Building Regulation standards and ensure they get a certificate from a Competent Person scheme such as FENSA or Local Authority Building Control.

Therefore, if whilst undertaking the refurbishment of your property you decide to change windows and doors changed to uPVC units, or upgrade the old one, there are two ways about it. You can purchase them from a firm who will supply and fit them; in this case they will issue you with a certificate from their regulatory body FENSA. However, this will cost you more than if you buy them on a supply only basis and get your carpenter to fit them. In this case you will not get a certificate. But as mentioned the valuer will request a certificate, what you need to do here as an alternative is when you submit your building notice ensure that it includes 'replacement windows and doors' on your description of work. If you do this then the Building Regs completion certificate will cover this item for you. If however your works are not covered by Building Control, you will have to buy your windows on a supply and fit basis to secure the FENSA certificate.

There is another alternative, but this tends to apply if the uPVC windows and doors are obviously new. I recently sold a property that had uPVC windows and they had been changed before I bought it, nothing new there as properties have had uPVC windows renewed for over 20 years now. The purchaser's valuer asked for a FENSA certificate, but I didn't have one. As I have used the same solicitor for over 10 years, it was not difficult for her to check the file that she prepared when I purchased the property approximately 3 years ago, she found that she had requested an 'Indemnity Policy' from the sellers solicitor. What the solicitors can do here is advise the lenders that the windows and doors are not a recent addition and that to cover it off they obtain an 'indemnity policy', a small insurance policy which usually costs around £25, and if there are any other anomalies, like missing old DPC, guarantees they can go under this same 'policy'. But, only if the work is historical not new.

Mike's top tip!

When it comes to selling your property make sure you have all the 'Pieces of paper' - that is certificates of conformity, Building Regulations Completion Certificates, Certificates of Lawful Use, FENSA Certificate and DPC and Timber treatment guarantees. These are essential to ensure a smooth sales transaction and that you get paid.

CHAPTER 5

The Party Wall Act 1996

Chapter 5. The Party Wall Act 1996

The Party Wall Act came into force on July 1st 1997 throughout England and Wales and becomes relevant to you if you:

- Work on a an existing wall or structure shared with another property
- Build a free standing wall or a wall of a building up to or astride the boundary with a neighbouring property
- Excavate near a neighbouring building

If you are intending undertaking any of the above work you must notify (in the required manner) any affected neighbours.

The act intends to provide a framework for preventing and resolving disputes in relation to work being carried out on a boundary wall, excavations near a boundary or adjacent building.

Adjoining owners can agree or disagree with what is proposed, where there is a disagreement, the Act provides for the resolution of disputes.

Section 1 of the Act refers to works if you plan to build a party wall or party fence or a wall astride the boundary line, you have no right to simply go ahead and build on the party wall or boundary, you must as described below serve a notice describing what you intend doing, the rule applies also if you intend to build up against the party wall.

Section 2 of the Act refers to work proposed on an existing party wall and lists works that the building owner has the right to do, which are:

- To cut into a wall to take the bearing of a beam or insert an DPC
- To raise the level of the wall
- To demolish and re build
- To underpin the whole wall
- To install a flashing

Section 6 of the act refers to work where you intend excavating new foundations for a new building or structure where the following may apply:

- You intend excavating a foundation within 3 metres of a neighbours building where your excavation will go deeper than your neighbours foundations.
- You intend excavating a foundation within 6 metres of a neighbours building where your excavation will cut through a line drawn downwards at an angle of 45 degrees from the bottom of your neighbours foundation.

This section may seem a little complicated so I will give an example from when I built a bungalow between two existing houses at the end of this chapter.

So, If you intend to do any of the foregoing works you must notify the owners of the adjacent property by serving a notice (an explanation of the work proposed and a time frame). If you do not and the neighbour objects to the work they can obtain a court order; however the only influence they can have is how and when the work is done, they can not stop you.

A notice, should be issued to the neighbour in writing at least 2 months prior to you commencing the work and should include your name and address, a clear description of the nature of the work and reference to the relevant part of the Act, Plans if applicable and finally the proposed start date.

Hopefully if you have a reasonable neighbour and you have approached the matter in a mature manner you should not have problems; however, life just isn't that simple! Particularly, if you have just bought a property and are new to the neighbour. In the event that your neighbour objects to the work, you need to appoint an 'agreed surveyor' who will draw up a document that states much the same as you were advised to provide previously, however as an Independent person they will ensure that the procedure proposed is fair to both parties.

You must pay the cost of the surveyor, and hopefully the neighbour will respect the independent person, but, again life just isn't that simple. If your neighbour doesn't accept the appointment of the surveyor, you must appoint a surveyor to represent the neighbour, and pay for him too. As a professional he should look objectively at your proposals and make recommendations in order to protect their interests. If, the neighbour is still not happy he may as mentioned apply to court for an injunction, but as you have done everything in a correct manner, it is highly likely that the court will rule in your favour and allow you to continue. But it's the hassle and delays!

As mentioned, under the act your neighbour cannot stop you doing this work, only influence you how and when. And how you should ensure that any damage you may cause will be rectified. There are no enforcement procedures for failure to serve a notice, however if you commence work without complying with the act your neighbour may seek an injunction through the courts to stop you working or seek other legal redress.

Case Study: Bryn Lodge.

I purchased a house at auction, which came with a plot where the owner had applied for and obtained Outline Planning Permission for a bungalow in the rear garden. The long rear garden originally had a garage served off that rear road, a formal road where there were half a dozen houses built over the years on the same side and a typical Welsh terrace on the other side of the road.

To one side of the plot someone had built a house approximately 20 years ago and their side path was tight to the boundary, on the other side of the plot was a poorly built stone and concrete block wall with a timber fence forming the boundary of the properties. The neighbouring bungalow was four metres away from the boundary.

On a bright sunny day, I thought I would pop along to see my building plot and give some thought as to when I was going to start building.

My 'Reserved Matters' Planning application had been submitted some weeks prior and I was awaiting approval so that I could start the work.

During the renovation works of the donor house I had excavated in the rear garden and connected a drainage pipe to the existing drains and run the pipe up the garden in readiness for the bungalow.

On my arrival at the plot, a lady from the existing bungalow was there talking to her neighbour. Excellent, I thought, a chance to introduce myself, assure her that when I would be undertaking the project I would ensure that the guys on site would be courteous and that we would be respectful of them. I said a polite hello, and told her my name and that I had bought the plot and would be building there soon, If I did! She flew at me....'you won't be building anything there, over my dead body, I'm not going to be run out of my own home' Wow, I thought, where has this come from. I noticed that I was standing on higher ground than her as her path was a metre below me, so I crouched down and attempted to understand her position, 'I don't understand' I said, 'I have no intentions of making life difficult for you at all, in fact I was just going to say that I will be respectful of your property throughout the build'

'I'm going to ring my husband' she said. I could see this lady was visibly shaking and on the edge of tears. I moved from where I was to the front of the site and stood on her path to be level with her, she ranted at her husband on the phone, and I heard her say, 'he's here standing on the drive', I immediately thought I've got my hands full here, so, to ensure that I couldn't be accused of anything, I backed off her drive and stood a couple of metres away from her, I anticipated that she would hand the phone to me so she would have to come to me. She gave me the phone, and I politely and calmly said to the guy, 'Hi, I'm Mike, I'm really sorry if I seem to have upset your wife, I can assure you that I only introduced myself by my name and that I was the owner of the plot', his response was. 'you won't be building anything on there, you don't have planning permission, you won't get it, so there is no point me speaking to you'.

I was gobsmacked at the arrogance and ignorance of this fella, 'Ok' I said, 'no problem, Good bye' and gave the phone back to the lady. I then just walked away.

You see this guy couldn't have been more wrong, the plot had outline planning permission, this is the consent to build. Following an outline consent you must (if you intend building in accordance with the proposals approved) submit a 'reserved matters application', this in my case was the detailed drawing of the bungalow, how it would appear (plans and elevations), the materials that I intended to use, bricks etc. or rendered block work and the boundary treatment, fences etc. As long as my proposals were in line with the outline approval, the application would be approved.

So, over the next few weeks I would visit the site with my ground worker and discuss the project and the programme of the works, we would need to demolish the existing garage and start the foundations. So here I will describe the proposals:

The plot was 5.6m wide with both boundaries parallel, my bungalow was 5m wide with an overhang for the fascia of 100mm and a 100mm gutter either side. We would be within the boundaries by 100mm (4 inches) either side.

It is usual for a foundation trench to be 600mm wide (this is the size of a bucket on an excavator, that, and a 300mm bucket), a cavity wall is in the order of 300mm therefore the projection of the foundation outside the wall is 150mm. Therefore I would be excavating overall 5.3m in width, giving myself 150mm (6 inches in old money) spare.

From the above, you will have deduced that under the Party wall act section 6 I will have been excavating within 3m of one neighbours foundations and within 6 metres of the other property (the troublesome neighbour).

Nevertheless, once the expected Planning permission was received and my building regulation application submitted, I arrived at the site with the excavator and the agitated lady immediately came out and said that we could not do anything on the site as they had spoken to their solicitor. And he had written a letter. Oh, really I thought, I can't start excavating on my own site, because your solicitor said so!. No disrespect to solicitors, but over the years I have dealt with a fair few. Some I must say when it comes to construction do have a clue, others unfortunately haven't. In my capacity as an Architectural practice owner I have provided expert advice to solicitors for various cases and have realised that their knowledge of construction is sometimes limited.

I proceeded regardless, only to have the chap arrive an hour or so later, looking for an argument. I politely reminded him that he once said that he had nothing to say to me, and that I was quite happy with this. He referred to his solicitors letter, so I politely advised him that once I had received it I would give it the attention that it deserved!

I return home to find the said letter, It advised me that he represented both the neighbours and that (and remember that he had not been to the site, seen it, or knew anything about it) under the Party Wall Act 1996 that I should not proceed with any work until I had served the requisite notice. No mention of what section of the act, just 'the Act'. He should of course be referring to Section 6.

So here was my response,

Dear Mr Solicitor,

Many thanks for your letter dated .....with regard to the above.

It appears that you have been briefed by your clients, and no doubt they have advised you of my proposals. Unfortunately, your clients appear to be against any development on this plot despite the fact that I purchased it with Outline Planning permission from the previous owner and the fact that they both have built houses on plots in a similar manner, albeit sometime prior.

Once I purchased the plot, I took it upon myself to introduce myself to your clients and assure them that as an experienced developer that I would respect their privacy and their property at all times.

Your letter requests that in accordance with the Party Wall Act 1996, that I serve notice on your clients providing them details of the proposals. You will be aware that had I needed to serve notice, that the act does not permit your clients from stopping me from building, but would ultimately merely cause me a delay, however you have failed to fully understand the proposals and the relevance to Section 6 of the act.

I would respectfully draw your attention to section 6 of the act, and would confirm that where I intend to excavate is within 3 meters of one of your client's buildings. As this building was constructed within the last 20 years and would have been constructed under the supervision of the Building Regulations Officer, it is anticipated that the foundations of your clients building will be in the order of the minimum of 900mm from ground level, the proposed depth of my proposed foundation will also be 900mm, therefore it is not intended that my proposed foundation will go 'deeper' than those of your clients property.

Turning now to your other client's property, their house is 4 metres from the boundary, the act states in section 6 that if I propose to excavate near a neighbour's property within 6 metres, then a notice is required if the depth of my foundation may pass through a cut line of 45 degrees taken from the bottom of their foundations. Assuming that their house has been constructed in accordance with the Building Regulations and in a good fashion, (unlike their boundary wall) it can be safely assumed that the depth of their foundation would be in the order of 1m, therefore providing I do not excavate more than 5m in depth, which I will not, Section 6 of the Act does not apply here either.

May I therefore, respectfully suggest that in future, prior to firing off a letter quoting non-compliance with an Act, instructing one to stop a project and incorrectly advising your clients, that you fully verse yourself with the facts of the project and more so of the relevant content of the Act itself.

I would be most grateful if you would advise your clients of your incorrect advice and advise them that I will be continuing with the project in accordance with the Planning approval No. 2013/xxx and the Building Regulation Approval Plan No. xxxx.

I would also be grateful if you could re-assure your clients that I have many years of experience in undertaking such projects and that I have every intention of completing the project in a proper manner.

I will ensure that the work is undertaken strictly within the boundaries of the plot, there is no need for me to have access from either of your client's property and would request that equally they respect my property and cease to interfere further.

I look forward to hearing from you.

Yours Sincerely

Mike Woods

MCIAT ACIOB

Needless to say, I did not have the courtesy of a reply.

So, again, what I am sharing with you is that in order to undertake various projects in accordance with the various approvals, regulations and Acts it is important that you know the content to ensure what is and isn't relevant to you.

Mike's tip!

When undertaking a project make sure you know what rules and regulations you need to comply with - get educated. Knowledge is Power.

CHAPTER 6

Typical Defects

Chapter 6. Typical Defects

This Chapter brings to your attention the main defects that you will come across when viewing properties in the UK and that most defects can be rectified.

Subsidence.

This is the term given when part of a property has lost the support of the ground on which it is built; if a house is built on ground with different quality soil the softer area will compress more that the firmer material, this will cause the foundation to crack and the walls above will drop.

When constructing a new home or extension the Building inspector needs to inspect the ground prior to pouring the foundations to ensure that the quality of the ground is consistent. If an area of the excavation is soft, the soft material will need to be excavated until better bearing soil has been reached.

In new build properties defects become apparent within a few months, particularly ground movement. With established houses (over 10yrs) if subsidence occurs it will be because of recent changes in the soil below, in this case we need to ask what has changed such that subsidence has occurred.

Normally houses will be constructed off a foundation, as mentioned above and the excavation should have reached a consistent layer of soil usually above 900-1200mm deep. In the UK we tend to hit clay at this depth, unless of course it a reclaimed site where other methods of foundation are employed. Clay or boulder clay is hygroscopic (it absorbs water) but uniformly, so in summer it dries out slightly and in winter absorbs moisture, but this uniform movement under the continuous concrete foundation has no adverse effect.

So, how does a house that is established house become affected? Well it usually comes down to changes in the moisture content of the ground which is localised.

Common culprits are trees within 3 metres and leaking drains. Let's look at the effects of trees first, you may be looking at a house which has a boundary with established trees or a tree may have been planted in the garden as a feature. However trees send out their roots searching for water and this takes moisture from the ground and as the roots extend and the trees grows they take more and more water from the ground around the foundations.

This localised absorption causes the soil to contract and if the tree is located near a corner of the property the foundation can crack and begin to move, sometimes only millimetres, but this movement will be evident in the brickwork or Blockwork of the house, with the crack initially following the joints in the masonry but as the movement continues cracks will show in the middle of bricks and blocks.

The main trees to be concerned about are: Oak, Ash Sycamore and Willow.

With regard to leaking drains, what happens here is that it is a knock-on effect. An old clay drain pipe which traditionally had cement joints can over time become porous and water from the roof (storm water) or water from the sinks and toilets (foul water) can start to leak into the ground. This localised saturation can cause the soil to 'wash away' under the foundation leaving a void where over time the foundation can drop leaving the wall above unsupported and prone to cracking.

If you are looking to purchase a property that has suffered from subsidence it can be rectified by a process called 'under pinning' this is where sections of the ground under the existing foundations are excavated and new deeper foundations are poured. Of course the cause of the initial problems needs to be addressed first. If the property is of facing brick then making the area look aesthetically pleasing will prove to be difficult unless you are able to render over the walls. If the walls were originally rendered then this is far easier to blend in.

You should seek advice from your insurance company or broker about their position with regard to subsidence, and make enquiries from the vendor whether there have been any previous claims for subsidence.

Anyone who wants to insure having made a claim would almost certainly have to seek help from a specialist as most firms are reluctant to take on a known subsidence risk.

Mike's tip!

Consider the property fully, it's easy to get carried away in the excitement - you may end up having difficulty selling the property on.

Rising Damp, Damp, Dry Rot, Wet Rot, Woodworm and Condensation.

Rising damp is where moisture from the ground moves upward into the structure by what is known as capillary action, and becomes apparent in the lower parts of the wall above skirting level. The moisture effectively dissolves salts from the wall construction and is drawn to the surface of the walls; when the moisture subsequently evaporates this leaves behind salt deposits which is known as 'efflorescence'. In addition this excess moisture within the property can lead to condensation, where the moisture evaporates into the air only to condense on the walls in other locations when the temperature drops.

The damaging effects of dampness in the structure and on the surface can lead to decay of the timber joists, skirtings and from dry rot, wet rot and timber infestation by woodworm. The continual damp conditions if not treated will lead to the growth of mould causing further damage to the structure.

Properties that were constructed before we started building properties using cavity walls, quite often in solid walls a damp proof membrane (DPC) was not installed, something that is fundamental in modern construction. So how do we go about getting this done? Well, we need to introduce a moisture barrier and most commonly this is done by specialists who inject a chemical solution by drilling holes into the wall at a specified distance apart and approximately 150-175mm above the outside ground level and then injecting a solution that creates a uniform barrier within the wall.

Due to the salts I mentioned earlier being drawn out of the structure these will have affected the internal render and plaster skim, so it will be necessary to hack off the internal plaster, usually to a height of 1 metre. Once the DPC has been installed and the wall given some time to dry out it can be re-rendered usually with a water proofer and then skimmed flush to match the wall.

The specialist will provide you with a guarantee provided by the manufacturer of the products and is underwritten on the basis that the installer has undertaken the work in accordance with their instructions. Again, when you come to sell your project the purchasers solicitor will ask for the guarantee if you state that you have had this work done.

Alternatively a physical DPC membrane, a plastic material supplied in rolls 100-600mm wide can be used, this will involve removing sections of the wall and the DPC being installed. This method can be very labour intensive and hence expensive but it is a more thorough method.

Dampness within a building usually occurs where the walls are of a solid construction, these walls are often constructed of stone or solid brickwork and finished externally with a sand cement render whether smooth finished or dashed with small stones. Moisture/ rain water enters the structure through cracks that have occurred over the passage of time; what happens is that rainwater enters the structure via the cracks and with capillary action water is pulled in further; the water soaks the structure and through gravity drops to the lower sections. Where the render is not defective at the lower level it is unable to escape and evaporate, and is therefore drawn inside the property.

Over time structure will become saturated and in Winter the water can freeze. The expansion of the water will cause the render to be pushed off the wall and the cracks increase in size; ultimately the render will become hollow and start falling off.

Other causes of dampness in walls can be where the rainwater gutters are leaking at the joints or have perished over time, where the running outlet has come away from the downpipe or where a downpipe has broken along its length. This continual saturation of the wall will cause problems as above.

Another not so obvious problem, which I have experienced is where the roof felt or membrane has rotten and does not extend into the gutter as it should. Believe it or not concrete roof tiles over time become porous so even if you haven't got a loose or missing tile rainwater can get under the tiles and this water drops onto the roofing felt and runs down to the gutter. Over time the water can rot the felt and the water can discharge into the wall; evidence of this can be seen when water literally drips off a window head. To remedy this it is necessary to strip back 3 or 4 layers of tiles, remove the battens and either install a new section of roof felt or a 600mm wide piece of damp proof membrane, tucked under the existing felt and extended into the getter, then install new battens before re-fitting the tiles.

Chimneys can be a real problem, having initially been built to perform a function, two as a matter of fact. One to allow the escape of smoke from a traditional fire, and also to allow the house to ventilate. As time passed and the use of boilers became more prevalent the old chimneys became redundant. Whereas in winter the chimney would have been dried out by the fire, without the heat over time these structures draw moisture into the wall. In addition, lead trays and flashings become porous, slip out in bad weather and allow moisture to pass through into the structure.

When this happens it can be quite confusing, because the evidence of water penetration is often nowhere near the source, often you may find a damp patch halfway along a wall in the front or rear room and not directly associate it with a leaking or defective chimney. Also, often the rafter closest to the chimney wall may well be touching the wall and water will track across and then run down the rafter. The water can start to drip off the rafter at any point producing a damp patch on the ceiling and wall.

So, if you are faced with this situation, you will need to go up into the loft space and inspect the chimney from the inside, it will be quite apparent as there will be clear evidence of where the water has been running, if not obvious if you inspect during a down fall.

Dampness in cavity walls can be due to the breakdown of the DPC and issues within the cavity. Cavity walls became more popular in the 1920s. Walls were built predominantly of 2 skins of brickwork with a cavity between of about 50mm (2 inches). The two skins were and still are constructed using wall ties, metal bars of varying shape. In the day attention to ensure that the ties were cleaned as the wall progressed was not as it is today and as the wall was built mortar would drop into the cavity and land on the tie; a build-up of mortar would effectively 'bridge' the cavity and water would track across, giving rise to damp patches over the wall.

In addition, to make matters worse, in the 80's the first round of thermal efficiency measures began and by filling the cavity with what was perceived water resistant material helped the water collect on the ties.

Later these ties would start to corrode, expand and start cracking the wall letting more water in. More on this in the section on Wall Tie Failure.

Dry Rot also known as Surpula Lacrymans is a wood destroying fungus that is present in timber that is damp and it is able to travel through the other building materials and break out and spread quickly. The timber may have become damp due to issues mentioned above or due to leaks from within the property, leaking shower trays, defective wall tiling which allows water from over bath showers to run down and under the bath, bath or shower traps leaking. Many of these you will be oblivious to until you start opening things up. Timber that has been affected will have shrunk and darkened and a fruiting body will appear which look like small pancakes with wide pores, you will also see a grey to light brown skin that can be peeled like a mushroom and a cotton wool like growth.

Dry rot can cause major structural damage and it is recommended that this is treated by a specialist who will require all the affected areas are exposed and if you are doing the work yourself or have a builder on board, you will need to remove all of the timber that has been affected as timbers buried into a wall or that are uptight against a wall will not be able to be treated, so need to be removed.

Wet Rot.

There are two types of wet rot, White and Brown. The most common is Coniophora Puteana – Brown rot and is known as cellar fungus. The mycelium (the vegetable part) looks like a dark Brown sheet like growth. Again like Dry Rot it can severely affect the structural integrity of the timber as it spreads and feeds on the cellulose of the timber.

Wet rot occurs in areas of high moisture content which allows the fungus to establish. To arrest the problem the source of the high moisture content must be addressed and removed, the defective timber removed and the area treated by a specialist.

Woodworm and other wood boring insects.

As mentioned above, if you have damp issues you've probably got a woodworm problem. Signs of woodworm are small holes about 1- 1.5mm in diameter and when live there will be a light brown powder, which is the faeces around the holes. The adult beetles lay eggs on/in the timber and the grub then feeds on the moist timber; this infestation can cause problems with structural timbers such as rafters, ceiling joints and floor joist. Treatment once you have resolved the other damp issues is quite straight forward, the timbers in the house need to be sprayed with an Insecticide, floor boards need to be lifted and all other areas where there is evidence of the woodworm. Usually the house needs to be left for 24 hrs to allow the chemicals to dissipate. Again you may want the specialist treating the damp issues to undertake the treatment for which you will receive a guarantee. Otherwise you can use a product called 5 Star which is made by Cuprinol which I often use and is applied with a low pressure spray gun. This product is also used to treat Dry Rot and Wet Rot

Condensation

This occurs when warm moist air comes into contact with cold surfaces such as walls and windows. On windows it is quite apparent and of course usually windows are colder than walls, however condensation does occur on walls and if the property is not ventilated properly this constant dampness can cause the plaster to delaminate off the walls and lead to Wet and Dry rot.

I find condensation is at its worst in some older terraced properties where the tenants and the families simply do not 'manage' the house properly. In one house that I had owned for a number of years, I had never had any real damp problems, but when a couple moved in and after a few months they started to complain about a light green mould appearing on the side of a wardrobe and dark patches on the walls at high level where the wall meets the ceiling, particularly in the corners of the rooms. But the main issue was water on the bathroom window which was streaming and the window's cill had puddles of water; these symptoms are typical of condensation. I arranged to visit them and I could feel the dampness in the air as the heating wasn't on even though it was November. They showed me the black patches and the puddles of water on the bathroom cill.

I couldn't understand where all the moisture was coming from; if there was a leak on the roof or rising damp, this would increase the moisture content in the house, but there was no evidence of this. All the windows were closed, I told them that they needed to open the windows if only a few millimetres and put the heating on, they looked at me as if I was stupid! "What, Let all the heat out"? They asked. I told them that they needed to heat and ventilate the house. I confirmed that moisture was not coming into the house, it was from within the house.

A week or so later they called me again, and I returned to the house, and all became apparent. When I arrived they had all their washing hanging on one of those pull-out lines which was extended across the landing, I hadn't noticed it before because when not in use it retracts into the wall. There were towels dripping, they hadn't been spun enough in the washing machine and on the floor in the bathroom the guy's jeans were soaking in a large plastic bin.

When I saw this I asked them, where did they think all the water from the drying process was going? They just didn't get it; the problem is that that amount of moisture in a house, not being ventilated or heated will over a short time cause problems with the plaster. Some of the wallpaper was starting to peel off the walls, and this may lead to other Wet and Dry rot issues.

I often find that in October and November, I may get a call off tenants saying that all of a sudden they have symptoms of condensation, which they simply refer to as damp. It can happen when the weather changes and there is heavy rain.

The best I can describe it is as follows: I'm sure that at one time you have been in the car with perhaps more than 2 people, in the evening and it starts to rain, the next thing that happens is the windows 'steam up'. So you turn the 'air vents' on, or you put the air conditioning on. Well, what has happened? Nothing inside the car has apparently changed to cause the windows to steam up, it's the fact that the rain outside the car has cooled the windows to the point where the warm moist air in the car, changes form a 'gas' to a 'liquid', I'm sure we all remember that from our physics lessons in school.

Well its exactly the same in a house, a stone box, filled with moist air from every day activities, boiling kettles, boiling potatoes and pasta on the hob, running hot baths and showers, and worst of all placing your towels on the radiators to dry. If you don't ventilate and heat, this moisture will 'condensate' on the windows and walls.

Evidence of condensation can be Black spots and patches in corners of rooms and behind furniture, particularly wardrobes, and green mould on leather and wood.

Where properties have been left unattended and high levels of moisture have occurred due to water penetration, condensation is the easiest defect to resolve, as the build-up of moisture will be vastly reduced once you have tackled the other issues mentioned and commenced drying the property out, even hiring a dehumidifier.

I recall some years ago when working in the Architects department for a Local Authority in the 80's I managed one particular refurbishment scheme of over 40 houses where the work included the replacement of timber windows with uPVC units and the cavity walls were injected with blown mineral wool.

After a few weeks the council tenants were complaining en mass that they were experiencing 'damp' problems in the houses and blamed it on the cavity insulation, when in fact what was happening, was whereas previously the moisture generated from their activities as mentioned previously, boiling kettles, and hanging clothes to dry on the radiators etc was being extracted through 'natural' ventilation from the ill-fitting timber windows, now they had new windows with seals the houses were not being ventilated and black spots began to appear in the corners of the room and their clothes started to go mouldy. So instructions were issued to open windows, use the trickle vents or use the night latch to maintain constant ventilation and to keep the heating on a low setting.

Cavity Wall Tie Failure.

As mentioned above, cavity walls were constructed using metal 'ties'. Straps known as fishtail or Butterfly were laid across the two skins, usually approximately 3 foot (900mm) apart horizontally and 18-24 inches vertically (450-600mm); at the time these were metal whereas today they are either galvanized steel of Stainless Steel, so over time these ties begin to rust and fail.

So, if you notice horizontal cracks approximately 450-600mm apart, then the likelihood is the wall is suffering from wall ties failure.

In order to address this defect you will need to employ the services of a specialist, The Building Research Establishment (BRE) set guidance for surveyors to determine the level of corrosion once inspected from level 1 to 9, and determined the severity where level 9 is very rusty and in need of urgent repair.

To determine the condition of the old ties they are located using a metal detector and holes drilled into the wall at various locations and a boroscope is used to view the ties. Once the condition is determined the surveyor will prepare a report and quotation to remove all the old ties and install new.

The work involved to remedy the situation is such that all the old ties need to be located and removed, or isolated, and new ties installed. There are various ties available today Mechanical, Helical Screw-in or Resin; the prices are similar, it's just a matter of which system your specialist uses. The new ties will be installed in the frequency determined by the current building standards which is 450mm vertically and 900mm horizontally and the holes filled with sand and cement or dashing to match the existing finish if you are intending on re-rendering.

If you do not re-render, the house will look like pretty awful, and besides it is highly likely that the render has become hollow due to the rain as explained previously, so if you are assessing a house and suspect wall tie failure you should allow for it to be hacked off and re-rendered, which will require scaffolding.

Japanese Knotweed

Whilst Knotweed is not a defect as such, its presence can severely affect the value of your project if it is not identified by you when purchasing a property. If you do not know what Japanese Knotweed looks like, just do a simple search on the internet, but I will run through the main issues of it here for you.

Japanese Knotweed is an invasive species of plant which can cause damage to properties if left untreated, particularly with drains and other buried services, paths and driveways, boundary/retaining walls, outbuildings, conservatories and gardens. The underground rhizomes (roots) of this species can penetrate loose aggregate and asphalt/concrete through small openings and voids. Once established, the rhizomes can expand with enough force to cause structural damage. Roots can exploit existing cracks and gaps in the drainage pipes in their search for water, which will further damage and, in some cases, result in the drains having to be renewed.

As a matter of interest, it was introduced to the UK in the 1800's as an ornamental plant and has simply taken over some areas.

Mortgage lenders will expect the presence of Japanese Knotweed to be noted on a residential valuation report as the RICS (the governing body for Surveyors and Valuers) guidance requires the valuer to indicate the presence of 'invasive vegetation'.

According to the Environmental Agency's 'The Knotweed Code of Practice', Japanese Knotweed rhizomes can extend up to 7 metres from the last sign of visible growth. Therefore this has been used as the minimum distance in the assessment process for valuers. If Knotweed is identified more than 7 metres away and, say, in a neighbour's property then the surveyor will still report on its presence and the particular lender will take a view on their position whether to lend depending on their policy.

Apparently there is no blanket policy from lenders which prevents them from lending on properties which have Japanese Knotweed, although because of the potential damage it can cause to properties and the difficulty in treating knotweed evidence is that there is some reluctance to lend.

Individual lenders will take into account a range of factors when considering when to lend on a property, taking into account the specific circumstances and some lenders consider applications on a case-by-case basis. Where remediation works are being implemented to remove Japanese Knotweed, generally lenders look for evidence of an initial treatment together with a commitment for an on-going four year treatment program.

So, if you are looking to buy a house as refurbishment and flip, then you will have little to no knowledge of your potential buyer's lender's policy on the presence of knotweed. It is therefore suggested that the risk in this case is too high.

However, if you are considering a house and have identified Knotweed which is not that severe you may want to reconsider it, if you are in a position to make a cash purchase. Many people will correctly be reluctant to buy such a property and as mentioned may well struggle to get a mortgage. This will clearly affect the value of the property as the vendors will struggle to sell.

Knotweed can be eradicated provided you embark on a program of treatment with Chemical control, by the use of specialised herbicides to plants over a period of several growing seasons. The cost of such treatment can be between £3,000 and £5,000 for a typical three-bedroom semi-detached house and can take more than three years to be effective.

From experience, properties for sale with Knotweed infestation are offered for far more than £5000 below market value and it is quite possible that you would be able to negotiate a further reduction in the price as a result and as a 'cash buyer'. So, depending on your financial position and attitude to risk, a property with a relatively mild case of infestation may prove to be a bargain.

Mike's tip!

Don't under-estimate the cost involved in putting building defects right or cut corners by not doing the work properly, often enough they will get noticed by the vendor or their Surveyor.

Property Inspection Check List

When you go to view a house it is better to have a check list with you so that you can easily and methodically go through the property as it's easy to get distracted whilst engaging in conversation with the agent over how long the property has been empty or how long it's been on the market etc. I have put together a list here of what you should be looking for. I have focused on the type of things that will occur on properties that you may be looking at towards the bottom end of the investment scale, the ones that will enable you to get your portfolio or investment plan rolling.

Check List.

External Inspection

Roof.

1. Ensure all the tiles are sitting evenly, and that there not any tiles missing.

2. Ensure that the ridge tiles are all in place and do not appear to be damaged and that the mortar joints are intact.

3. If there is a chimney, look to see that the lead flashings are all evenly fitting and flat against the brickwork and roof. If there are soakers check to see that they have not slipped out of position.

4. Check if the roof is sagging in the middle, this can happen if original slates have been changed for concrete tiles. Look at neighbouring houses to see if they still have the original slates roofs.

5. Check that the tiles extend into the gutters and that the tiles at the eaves are even and the eaves are sealed.

6. Check that the gutters and downpipes are in good condition; if they are not modern uPVC and not well fitting, consider replacing them. Check that the running outlet makes a good connection with the downpipe, ill-fitting connections can lead to penetrating damp in solid wall walls.

If there are a number of the above items that need attention, your builder Contractor or Roofing Contractor will be able to resolve all these. These types of 'repairs' can be accessed from a ladder, so there should be no need for scaffolding.

External Walls.

1. Rendered walls, look for any cracking, whether it be random or regular (refer to cavity wall ties failure), run a key lightly over the surface horizontally and vertically, any hollowness will be heard, which you can reaffirm by further tapping. Depending on the condition you will need to consider hacking off and re-rendering. This will need scaffolding.

2. Brickwork walls, as above check for cracking, in particular wall ties failure if the property is more than 40 years old; cracks located in corners and in area's above manhole covers can suggest localised subsidence.

3. Window openings, check that existing windows are sealed and that the seals have not perished. If the windows and doors are timber or aluminium, consider replacement. Some timber and aluminium windows fitted in the 1980's and 90's were double glazed, you may see that they have 'misted up' inside the units, this occurs as the double glazed units have lost the vacuum seal. If the frames are in good condition you can replace the double glazed units themselves. Albeit they will be far thinner than units fitted the new windows.

4. External ground levels, if the paths are above the level of the internal floor this can lead to dampness in the walls.

Internal Inspection.

As you may be inspecting houses that have solid stone walls, cavity walls, flats etc. I will try and cover all aspects, so apply whichever is relevant to you.

Walls.

1. If the property has been recently vacated and in good general order, you may find that the only issue may be condensation. If the property has been uninhabited for some time start by checking the skirtings and the external walls at low level; we are looking here for rising damp. I would recommend that you invest in a 'damp meter' for instant confirmation of dampness. Use the handle of a screwdriver and knock the walls, to check for hollow plaster. If the readings show that there is evidence of rising damp, you will need to have a DPC installed. And have the skirtings replaced.

2. Look for any areas where there is localised damp patches; if so depending on the wall construction there is a breach of the outer skin. If it's a rendered solid stone wall, check the condition of the render above the area of dampness, you may well have determined that the render is cracked and hollow, which will explain the internal damp. If the walls are cavity walls, a localised damp patch will suggest that the wall ties are tracking water across the cavity, so check for wall tie failure. It has been known for the cavity to have been filled with blown fibre of polystyrene beads, and small voids have occurred, which act as pockets for condensation to collect and then produce a damp patch randomly located on the wall. Check if the cavity walls have been retrospectively insulated. Houses post 1995 started to have Rockwool 'full fill' insulation installed which did not have this issue.

3. If inspecting a house and all the internal walls sound hollow and it is apparent that the walls are not solid, you may find that it is of a Timber Frame construction, Timber frame houses became popular on some developments in the later 90's, this was the early days of 'Timber Frame' construction. Starting in

one corner knock the external wall with the handle of a screw-driver, the response should be a 'solid' sound, then knock again 150mm away, the response will be hollow, keep tapping the wall moving further away from the corner, at anywhere between 400mm and 600mm the response should change to a more 'solid' sound again. If this is the case the house is Timber Frame.

In this event it is difficult to determine if the frame, over the years has been affected by any damp issues. These houses were usually finished with Brickwork on the outer skin.

4. If you note damp patches on the upper parts of the walls on the landing, typical in terraced houses, often it will be the chimney which is in the ownership of the adjacent house and may need attending to, re check this from the outside. Whilst not immediately apparent the joints in the brickwork may be poor and the chimney has become porous.

Timber Skirtings, and Floors.

1. Look for evidence of Dry and Wet Rot, the skirting will look shrivelled and the paint will have cracked. Use your screwdriver or a key and press against the timber, you may find it to be very soft, cardboard like. If this is the case the rot has more than likely travelled into the floorboards and joists. If the floor is covered with a carpet, pull it up from one corner and peel it back. Check for signs in the floor boards, you may also see small holes in the floor boards and a light brown dust, which will be wood worm as these defects are often seen together. Treating with a solution will remedy the problem; if the ends of the joist have been badly affected then they will need to be replaced. This is often common on older terraced houses on the ground floor front and rear walls, but not so common at first floor level, but still check as poorly sealed cills can cause water to track into the wall and dampness can affect the floor construction.

2. Bathrooms are often an area where rot issues can be found even in houses that appear in relatively good condition. Over time, with the tiles around the bath, other than the more obvious

silicon seal leak movement in the structure and the moisture from an over-bath shower will cause the grout to crack. Once water starts to run into cracks a process called capillary action causes it to form a small stream and the water will 'pull' through soaking the plasterboard or wall behind. To check if this has happened, pull the bath panel off the front of the bath and with torch check for damp patches and evidence of 'water runs' on the wall. You will find that the walls under the bath will not have been painted and still be Pink (if plastered) or just bare plasterboard, if the tiles have been leaking the plasterboard will be very soft. To remedy the problem you either rake out all the joints in the tiles or if you are looking to improve to sell, you may re-tile the bathroom. The other obvious area to check is behind the toilet, (not a nice area to be poking around) but, leaks from ill-fitting waste couplings or leaking flush pipes will cause havoc with the floor boards and joists.

Electric Circuit

1. The Electric fuse board is usually located near the front of the property often above the front door or in a cupboard in an alcove in the front room. The first thing you want to note is if it is a modern plastic box with a flap front cover - if this is what is there, the circuits may have been updated. The next thing you want to look for is a Yellow and Green cable approximately 5mm in diameter; this is the Earth cable, something that would not have been provided in early installations. If you do not see this cable or new box (Consumer Unit) you may well be looking at a Brown box with a row of about 4 or 5 circuit breakers with a single On/Off switch to one side. This will need to be replaced and the circuits either uprated or replaced.

   Old cables are thinner than those required to meet current standards and the older wires lose their ability to conduct electricity efficiently and will cause the fuses to 'blow' or 'burn out'. There are usually two circuits in a property, the lighting circuit and the power circuit. Sometimes the power circuit only has been upgraded, this may be evident by seeing surface mounted white trunking running to surface mounted power points. Whilst this may have been done, check the wires to the light fittings from the ceiling rose, if there are two thin twisted wires, the lighting circuit will not have been upgraded, which would have involved lifting a lot more floor boards and joining up the lighting circuit. If there is evidence of an old circuit you will need to upgrade partially or a full re-wire.

Central Heating System and Boilers

1. When inspecting the central heating system you may come across a couple of different systems. Most older systems had one of two systems - either a gas fire place with what is called a 'back boiler' typically called a 'Rayburn' these were good simple systems but inefficient, they would have utilised the original chimney of the house and there would be an aluminium liner inside to the flue terminal. These systems used air from the room to combust the gas so would need to have a vent located through the main wall of the house, letting cold air in! The other older system whether it be Gas or Oil would be a floor standing unit located in an out-house or in the kitchen. Both these systems are what are called 'indirect' where water is passed through the heating pipework and radiators and there would be a copper cylinder in a cupboard usually off the landing, this cylinder had a copper tube coiled inside and this would 'indirectly' heat the hot water. These systems also utilised an electric element in the cylinder called an immersion heater, to heat the water. You may recall either when you were younger or heard your parents refer the fact that they had to wait for the water to heat up before having a bath. These systems also had a cold water storage tank holding approximately 80-100 litres of water in the loft space, this tank of water provided the water pressure at the taps, known as 'head'. These tanks and pipes in the attic were prone to freezing in the winter months.

   These systems are very inefficient compared to new Condensing Combination Boilers used today, in addition the old radiators compared to the new are not as efficient in 'radiating' their heat.

I have had a number of houses with these systems and over the years have replaced them with new Combi's once the repairs became too frequent and the old radiators became 'pin holed' i.e. rusted.

If you are buying to rent and the system in place is functioning properly and you have a Gas Safe Engineers Safety Certificate, I would run with it until it becomes an issue. If you are buying to sell, I would most certainly replace the whole system. Most 2 to 4 bedroom houses will comfortably run off a Combi boiler. If the property is larger and has two bathrooms or more I would suggest that you install a 'Mains Pressured' System where there will be Boiler and a Hot water storage tank which is pressurised so that in the event that there is a bath being run, a shower and the washing machine at the same time there will be no noticeable drop in water pressure.

Below I have put together a chart where I have listed the various defects, the level of importance attached to them and the level of cost you should consider. The level of importance I have graded as if you are buying to let; it may not be important to do immediately, but more so if you intend buying to sell on. Also with regard to costs, I can't take account of the variance of costs across the whole country and I have used rates that I would expect to pay, so I have assumed that you will be either starting to build your property business or expanding your current portfolio by investing in relatively low cost areas of the UK. If you are using this book and are looking to invest in more expensive areas by all means add 10-20% to my estimated cost.

Legend.

Importance 1-10. 1 Being not very necessary to 10 being very necessary.

Costs. Every ★ represents £500 and -/+ means less than or more than.

Defect	Importance	Costs
Roof		
Overhaul roof – loose & missing tiles/ridge pieces	10	- ★
No roof felt – replace slate roof	10	★★★
Scaffolding	10	★★★
Overhaul Chimney	7-10	★
Removed Chimney (if defective & not required)	7-10	★ +
Overhaul Gutters and Downpipes	5-8	- ★
Replace defective Gutters and Downpipes	7-10	- ★
Replace defective fascias and barge boards	7-10	★
Walls		
Hack off defective render and re-render	8-10	★★★★
Scaffolding	10	★★★
Cavity wall tie failure	8-10	- ★★
Replacement windows and doors	8-10	★★★★★★
Internal		
Rising damp – DPC injection	10	★
Hack off and re-plaster 1m	10	★★
Wet Rot / Dry Rot	10	- ★
Electrical circuit – no earth	10	★ +
Electrical circuit – full rewire	10	★★★★
Replacement of Boiler	7-10	- ★★★
Replacement of Central Heating	7-10	★★★★★ +

CHAPTER 7

Property Investing and Letting

Chapter 7. Property Investing and Letting

Working out Yields

The beauty of property investing is the ability to leverage your money, in the UK we also call it gearing. Despite all the problems in the financial world you can still now get a mortgage secured against a property, therefore, you are using the bank's money to invest in order to make a profit. Some people do not believe in taking on debt, particularly the older generation, but if you are geared correctly. i.e. not borrowing too much against a property that is over-priced then you will do well out of it.

To determine whether a property is a good purchase compared to what rent you will receive, we use a term called 'Yield'. This is expressed as percentage based on the rental income less other costs annually divided by the value of your investment. For example, you put £60,000 in the bank for one year at 5% and they give you £3000 you will have receive a Yield of 5%

3000/60000 = 0.05 x 100 = 5%

Let's say you have found a house for £60,000 and you happen to have the money and you don't want to get a mortgage. Using the same structure as above.

You receive monthly rent for a property of £433 (£100 per week) which equates to £5196 less 10% for maintenance and another 10% for management fees, so minus £1039. You are in receipt of a net profit of £4157, you invested £60,000 of your own money.

4157/60000 = 0.069 x 100 = 6.9%

That explains Yield, when you start to leverage your investment we then have to start looking at Return on Investment, R.O.I

Return On Investment

Now let's assume that you are not averse to borrowing money and you borrow £45,000 at a rate of 5%, this will cost you £2250, and only invest £15,000 of your own money

You receive the same rent above of £5196 minus the other costs or allowances of £1039, and the cost of the loan £2250, leaving you with a profit of £1907,

1907/15000 = 0.127 x 100 = 12.7%

By doing this you still have £45,000 to invest in three more similar houses, therefore you will be making a constant profit of 12.7%. £1907 x 4 = £7628

£7628/60000 = 0.127 x 100 = 12.7%

So even though you are repaying the bank interest for the privilege of borrowing the money you now have a R.O.I of 12.7% as opposed to Yield of 6.9%

Make sense?

So, in order to start off your BTL property portfolio you really need to access between £10,000 and £15,000. Unless of course you manage to find yourself a lease option straight away, it's not impossible. As mentioned earlier there are property investors buying property without using any of their own money, but this is for the more experienced investors so lets' get you off the ground and we will delve further into more complex methods as we gain experience.

It was announced last year that the Bank of England had made money available to lenders for the sole use of lending to property buyers to get the housing market moving, evidence of which has appeared by way of more attractive mortgage products coming on the market. When we say 'more attractive', over the last few years we investors have been subjected to lenders arrangement fees of more than £2000 or 3% of the loan. Consider this against the products available to us in the 00's where applications were 'free', no application fee's, often there were free valuations and even 'cash backs' on completion. Oh! how it's changed.

The most common BTL mortgages provide a maximum of 75% of the valuation where available, recently some lenders are offering 80% LTV - Loan To Value. This means that on a typical £60,000 purchase you can now borrow £48,000, so your deposit will be £12,000.

Quick calculator

To help you make quick calculations when assessing a potential property, work on the basis that for every £20,000 you borrow your mortgage payment will be £100 per calendar month. This works out at a rate of 6%, whilst you can expect to secure rates of under 5%, so this amount will cover most of your monthly expenses also.

For example if you borrow £40,000 your monthly payment will be £200, for £60,000 it will be £300 and so on. If you have determined what rents you can demand for properties in this purchase price bracket, you can make a quick calculation to assess whether a deal will stack up or not.

Determining Your Market

All towns and Cities have a diverse rental market. Many regions are not very affluent and the levels of rents payable are not in the same league as say London or any other major City, but neither are property prices.

There are many regions where rent to property prices ratio are very good. I have in the book demonstrated that a R.O.I of more than 10% are possible for single lets. In London they are happy to receive 5-6%, but in the comfort that the properties are increasing in value.

For example, my solicitor partner over the last 15 years has been happy to buy 2 bedroom flats in the Surbaton and Ewell area and whilst he is achieving R.O.I of around 5%, he has found that every 4 years or so when he makes a purchase they have risen by £50,000. Current Prices are around £250,000. He is happy to invest £60,000 deposit now in the knowledge that the prices have historically risen such that the deposit is returned in 4-5 years.

If you were to start with your £15,000, and therefore a total purchase budget of £60,000, a search on Rightmove or Zoopla using the Postcodes in the less affluent areas will reveal pages of Mid Terraced Houses in various states of repair. Some will be in need of full modernization, some will have been modernised to a point.

It is this part of Investing that I find the most exciting, seeking out the property that works for me. If you are completely new to house buying you will be amazed at what you can come across. I recently viewed a house where it had not been touched for 50 years, the dear old lady had passed away. The interior decor looked like Hilda Ogden's lounge from Coronation St (I don't watch it honestly, just a childhood memory), there was an old 'Rayburn' Oven in the kitchen and outside at the bottom of the garden the 'Ty Bach'! (Ty bach means, little house in Welsh) that housed the toilet. I had to take a picture to show my Daughter, as she would never believe me.

If you have a little more at your disposal and raised your budget to £100,000, you may well find a more modern property, such as a bungalow or a 3 Bedroom semi in good order on the outskirts of Birmingham or Leeds for example.

A further increase in your budget could lead you into a better quality property and 'nicer' areas where you could find yourself looking at a 3 bedroom detached house somewhere. On this point, I would avoid being attracted to new developments; whilst on the face of it they are new, with no potential maintenance issues, you will not a get a great discount unless you buy a few, and they will be priced at the very top of the market. You may be lucky by picking up one of the very last few houses for sale on the site. At this stage the developer will want to close the show house and the site office and move on, you 'may' get a bargain. Right place and right time scenario.

Any of the properties above will suit the range of available tenants, whether they be tenants on Benefits, Private (employed) tenants, Students or Corporate (Individuals who are working for a large local company who are provided with accommodation as part of their job).

Your Strategy

Of course your overall goal is to improve your personal wealth, whether it be to increase your annual income so that you can become financially independent or provide for your long term financial security, or that of your children. The two main aspects of property investment are R.O.I (Return on Investment) cash flow and Capital Growth.

The following figures show the 'Net' Return On Investment. To calculate the actual N.R.O.I. you must take account of all the costs involved with the purchase. Some refer to this as the 'True Rate of Return'.

Net Return On Investment (R.O.I.)

£15000 Investment (25%)

£1700 Legal fees and House preparation

£60000 Purchase price

£45000 Mortgage (75%)

Repayments £45,000 x 5% (int rate) = £2250 pa - Monthly= £188.00

Rent	£433
Mortgage	£188
Management 10%	£ 43
Voids/Maint 10%	£ 43

Insurance	£10
Profit	£149 PCM
Annual Profit	£1788 (149x12)
N.R.O.I	£1788/16700 = 10.7%

Typical purchase costs for your solicitor will be £700 inc VAT; I pay £400 plus disbursements plus VAT. The cost of preparing your property will of course vary but for the exercise let's assume that you have to give the place a lick of paint and you renew a carpet here and there. As you can see I have allowed £1000.

Landlords Insurance is provided by specialists, you may have seen Direct line advertising on the TV, I use a broker and they seek 'best of market' quotes. As your portfolio grows you will add these new properties and build a block policy. Expect an annual premium to be around £120.

Using the figures above, we will add these costs to our initial £15,000 giving a total of £16,700.

In reality a N.R.O.I figure for year 1 can only be accurately calculated after the year, as after the year's letting period you will know if you have had any voids (periods where the house was unoccupied)

For the purpose of this exercise let assume that 3 weeks after you purchased the property you secured a suitable tenant and that tenant stayed for the 12 months. And within this period you carried out the painting and presentation.

Actual R.O.I for year 1

You receive the same rent above less £300 for the first 3 weeks void - £100 x 49 weeks = £4900 minus the other costs of £636 (but no void period or maintenance) and the cost of the loan £2256 leaving you with a profit of £2008

First year Profit 2008/16700 = 0.12 x 100 = 12%

At 12% this still represent a great return in the first year.

So whilst initially we allowed for a 10% buffer for maintenance and voids, if you prepared the property well before letting and ensure that you incurred no maintenance costs on the property and you get a good reliable tenant who remains in the property for the 12 months you should save yourself those costs. Moving forward, as your portfolio grows, so will your cash flow, and within that you should build up a slush fund for maintenance and voids.

To explain ROI in another way, it will take you approximately 8 years to get your initial investment of £16700 back, from then on you are making pure profit - in theory, but you never really see because as a serial investor you just keep ploughing on.

16700/2008 = 8.31 (yrs)

> ***Mike's top tip!***
>
> *Aim to build a portfolio of a minimum of 4 properties as soon as possible*

When you have one property and the tenant leaves after 6 months the mortgage will have to be funded from the first 6 months profit. If the property lies unoccupied for a second month, you will probably need to subsidise the mortgage. If you only have 2 properties the profits from the second house will subsidise the first, and so on. The more properties that you have the better chance you have of the income covering voids and maintenance and generating a decent profit from your portfolio. So, from my experience observing the difficulties new landlords experience the pressure is reduced once they have 4 or more properties.

I have known a few people to restrict their portfolio to just a couple of houses as they have a few problems early on, (buy not knowing how to manage the house and tenants properly) and not having expanded as they see more houses means more problems. So, low and behold they sell up and get out, saying renting property is not for them. So they are still stuck in their day jobs; if only they got themselves educated properly - they took action but through lack of guidance fell off the wagon. Such a waste, they will never know how their lives could have changed.

HMO's - Home of Multiple Occupation

Whilst I would advocate that to start your property journey you look at single lets, the more adventurous may determine that you want to go for an HMO, so what exactly is an HMO?

The Housing Act 2004 Section 254 defines an HMO as follows:

A Building or Parts of a Building where:

a. 'it consists of one or more units of living accommodation not consisting of a self-contained flat or flats;

b. 'the living accommodation is occupied by persons who do not form a single household

c. 'the living accommodation is occupied by those persons as their only or main residence or they are to be treated as so occupying it'

d. 'their occupation of the living accommodation constitutes the only use of that accommodation;

e. 'rents are payable or other consideration is to be provided in respect of at least one of those persons' occupation of the living accommodation; and

f. 'two or more of the households who occupy the living accommodation share one or more basic amenities

The benefits of an HMO are that as you are renting rooms or suites (room inc WC) in a single house to a number of people, the rent that they pay invariably includes the utility bills and as you are the owner you will pay the Council Tax, therefore the gross rent received will be far greater than a single let. My HMO's that were previously single lets have increased the cash flow by 280%.

What to Purchase

If you decide that this is the way you want to proceed you need to look for a house that can accommodate at least 4 individuals, the rooms may well be let on a single occupancy but most people will want a double room. There are minimum requirements for the size of a let-able room, I do have rooms in houses where they have a single bed as most houses have a 'box' room, as long as it meets the minimum requirements you will be able to let it. But the double rooms tend to go first and its only the LHA tenants that are more prudent who opt for a single room.

The room will need in addition to the bed a wardrobe and set of drawers or a combination wardrobe. We will try a provide a bedside drawers and side lamp.

The house must have at least one bathroom with WC and a kitchen, the size of the kitchen must be within the Local Authority guidelines but the typical kitchen in a 3 bedroom house is more than adequate.

The house will need to meet the Fire protection requirements to ensure the safety of your tenants, which will include fire doors, fire alarm system and compartmentation, which is providing fire protection to the ceilings and stairs.

Location

Depending on which sector of tenants you target the location of your HMO can vary. For example, if you wish to provide for Professionals working near the City, you will want to locate your HMO within walking distance of the Railway station and have shopping and food outlets within a short walk. This will negate the need for the tenants to rely on having a car. If you choose to target LHA tenants, then the focus on location will invariably be close to a town centre, again within walking distance. And then there are the students, obviously you need to be focusing on a property close to the college or University, again as close as possible.

I have one particular HMO which is for Professionals and is strategically located near to a town but more importantly a commercial business centre, where there are Insurance offices and solicitors offices.

Strangely from my research HMO's are not in demand near hospitals, the hospital tends to have on-site accommodation for nurses and doctors and other than that they tend to group together and take on a house share between themselves. Technically creating an HMO!

Acquiring your HMO

Most 'vanilla' BTL mortgage companies do not lend on HMO's as they are seen to be 'commercial' entities as opposed to domestic, in most cases you will need to establish a relationship with a commercial lender such as a Bank, but I must admit this will be difficult for you in your early stages because they will want to see that you have what they will call 'sector' experience before they extend you a line of credit.

The most popular way is to secure 'bridging finance' though again some lenders still want to see some kind of sector experience. These companies will usually lend you 70% of the purchase price and the term will be between 6 and 12 months. The finance is not cheap and can cost you anything from 8-12% per annum, plus admin and application fees.

Once you have got your HMO up and running you will need to arrange what is called 'back end' finance; your specialist mortgage broker will be able to place you. However if you attend the 'Property and Refurbishment Master Class' I will be able to introduce you to a lender and I will offer you my support in order to secure the finance.

As the HMO as mentioned is a commercial entity the finance you raise will now be based on the income that the 'business' produces as opposed to the 'bricks and mortar' value of the building The bank or finance provider will instruct a valuer and you should provide them with documentary evidence of your 'business' Income and expenditure, from this the valuer will use a factor of between 7 and 9 of the annual income to project the value. From this your funder may offer you a loan of 70%.

The beauty of the HMO model is that you may have invested £150,000 in your building and have say 5 let-able rooms at £400 per month. The annual income on this is £24,000, the valuer will allow an amount for outgoings as mentioned above. He may discount the figure above by 20% returning a figure of £19,200. If the valuer uses a factor of say 8 he will report to the funder that he values the business at £153,000. You will look to your funder to release to you 70% which will be £107,520

The lender in this case will invariably only offer a repayment loan, which is where over a nominal period of 20 years you repay all of the loan plus interest. For the purpose of the exercise I will use a rate of 7% the loan may be at a rate of around 4.3% over base (currently 0.5%), giving a rate of 4.8% currently. Using a rate for the purpose of this exercise of 7% of the loan, this gives a repayment of £7526.

Using the R.O.I formula for an HMO

Net income 24,000 – 20% for costs, less loan £7526 = £11,674

Investment 150,000- 107,520 = £42,480

R.O.I

11674/42480 – 0.274 x 100 – 27.4%

Have I got your attention?

In the UK you can usually convert a house into an HMO without Planning Permission, providing you do not create 6 or more rooms. If your HMO building is 5 rooms and 2 floors it will not need to be licensed by the Local Authority either. Even though you will still need to comply with the Local Authorities Environmental Health Departments minimum requirements as mentioned above.

Should your house be 3 floors or more (inc a basement) and 5 rooms (or more) and have shared facilities you will need to obtain a license from your EH Department, this license application will be issued providing they deem you to be a 'Suitable and Responsible' person to run the property. You can designate a letting agent to be your manager as ideally the 'responsible' person needs to be someone who will regularly inspect the property and ensure that regular maintenance is carried out.

If your HMO needs licensing your EH officer will carry out a Housing Health and Safety Rating System (HHSRS) risk assessment following which they will issue you with a schedule of work that you must comply with. The only main difference I find between my Licensed HMO's and Non Licensed HMO's is the different type of Fire detection system and emergency lighting requirements, as well as the need for more sanitary facilities for the additional tenants. The schedule of work will give you a period of time to undertake the work, I'm sure different councils will specify different periods but the Councils within the areas I operate in will usually require the work to be done in 6 months, some less important tasks-12 months.

Having to License your HMO is nothing to be feared, particularly as a responsible landlord you will want to ensure that you are providing the best facilities that you can. The license lasts for 5 years.

Mike's tip!

Converting a single let property to an HMO can increase your rental income by 280%

Key Elements that make a successful Buy To Let Property

Does it stack up (Financially)

By using the information aforementioned you need to assess if the property is profitable. You will need to research what the rents are in the locality that you are focusing on and assess this against the costs of the property.

Example:

Using the example above, you have found a 3 bedroom terraced house for £60,000, the rents locally for a 3 bedroom house are £433 per month. Based on the figures mentioned previously your monthly costs were £187.50 for the mortgage and £86 for management and maintenance, So this property 'Stacks up' showing a monthly positive cash flow of £159.

Always buy in an area where there is good demand for rental property.

The above property has a positive cash flow, however if it was located a mile or so outside a small town for example, on a quiet road the demand would be far less than a similar property within walking distance of the town. Both properties would attract a similar rent but you will find the property closer to shops and bus stops etc will be easier to rent out.

These are the key elements, however to really benefit from your new venture you need to seek properties that we refer to as BMV- Below Market Value. These are properties that are for sale by 'Motivated Sellers'.

The first example of a Motivated Seller is a Repossession company selling on behalf of mortgagees in possession. You will often see these properties by agents who are not local, they will have been given a property to sell as it has been repossessed and it will be advertised as 'Attractively Priced to Sell'. From your research you may note that it will be marketed at a price slightly below other similar properties.

Other Motivated sellers may be someone who needs to sell before they get repossessed, they may well be selling through a High Street agent or you may well find them by searching through Gumtree or even see a hand-made sign in the garden.

As you become more experienced by enrolling on the Mentoring program and by attending the network meetings I will show you how to find property that is up to 30% Below Market Value.

In addition, you will learn how to find out what the true market value of a property is and the maximum rent you could achieve.

Always try to Buy Below Market Value

Mike's tip!

*As someone who wants to 'profit' from your new business, the essence of making a profit is not when you sell something, but **when you buy it**. Buying at a discount should be your main aim.*

Case Study. Moorland Rd

I was recently approached by an existing tenant, asking if I was interested in buying a property. My response was 'Of Course' never discount anything that you are offered even if you are not in position at that point to proceed, there will be someone in your network group who may be, and will be more than willing to pay you a 'finder's fee'.

The seller was a friend of an existing tenant and as I was a 'good landlord' in her words, she felt that I would be fair with them.

I made arrangements to view the property but first I requested the address. I fired up the Internet, Google maps showed me the general area, and prices researched from Rightmove and Net house Prices showed me the recently sold prices in that street and the average price sold over the last 3 and 5 years. I also researched what the rent would likely to be.

Having done my 'due diligence', I was armed with some facts and it now remained to ensure that the house was in good order and to find out how much the seller wanted.

My research showed me that the average price over the last 3 years was £85,000, and over 5 years was £97,500. The larger average was due to a house selling at the end of the peak in 2008 for £109,000. This was nice to know, but my focus is on the more realistic figure of £85,000.

From my meeting with the seller I learned that he was nearing retirement age and his income was low. He had a small mortgage of only £10,000 but his wife had run up some credit card bills over the years of some £25,000. His monthly income was barely paying his bills, so needed to sell the house to pay off the bills.

Now this presented him with another great problem; once he had sold where was he and his family going to live? He had 2 teenage children in local schools so he wanted to stay local.

Whenever I do Property deals in these circumstance I am strictly ethical, by this I mean I do not dive in and take full advantage of the person's position and make them a derisory offer and tell them to take it or leave it. I try and work out a solution that is a Win -Win for both of us.

In an effort to provide an all-round solution, I suggested to the seller that if I did buy the house I could offer him a 3 bedroom property that I had available for him to rent. I suggested that if we agreed on a price that he could view the property I had with his family and 'IF' they were totally happy with it they could move straight into it. He agreed.

During our discussion he said that he would like around £55,000 for the house, I thought that this was fair and we agreed on the figures in principle and I left it with him to discuss with his family. We arranged for him to view my house and following the viewing he agreed to the whole deal.

In summary

I had purchased a house for 30% Below the Market Value the 75% mortgage on £55,000 would be £42,500, which would result in a monthly cost of £200 inc Insurance. The potential monthly rent was £475, giving a positive cash-flow of £275 PCM (£3300pa). Also I had agreed a tenancy for one of my houses for a year.

The initial Investment plus costs were £13,200- (deposit and legals) The ROI is 3300/13200 = 25%

If I keep the house for 10 years and then sold it, allowing a loss of 10% for voids and maintenance on the rent, and the house did not go up in value, I would have:

1. Received a rental income profit of £30,000 and 2. Made a profit of at least £30,000 on the sale. (Gross of CGT)

Overall taking account of my initial investment of £13,000 a gain of £47,000 in just 10 years.

Now I would like you to take a minute to consider this in your own circumstances. Let's say that you have a child who is between the ages of 7 and 10, I realise that it's very early days but, have you thought about how you would fund your child's education if they decided to that they wanted to go to University?

If you take action now and continue with me to learn How to Successfully Invest in Property, you will be in a far better position than if you don't do anything. Do you not agree?

Mike's tip!

Always keep your property options open, never discount anything until you have been to see it. Not everything will be suitable, but you won't know until you have given it full consideration.

CHAPTER 8

Capital Growth

Chapter 8. Capital Growth

Will property prices continue to rise?

Earlier in Chapter 1 we saw that over the last 50 years house prices have steadily increased; it is well documented that the boom that ended in 2007 saw an accelerated growth with property prices in some local areas more than doubling in value.

In real terms in 2001/3 I was regularly purchasing properties between £30,000 and £40,000. These were properties in good order, and ready to let. Those properties rose at their peak to somewhere between £80,000 and £95,000.

Today I would say that the values are typically £70,000 to £80,000, so as mentioned earlier a drop of around 20% from the peak but still an increase or 100% from the initial price.

In all Investment fields, you will hear that Historic evidence is all that can be used to 'predict' growth. If you took out an endowment policy 20 years ago, they would have told you 'based on previous years' growth' you can expect x% growth.

Unfortunately however, you will read in the small print when you come to cash in your underperforming policy that -'past performance is no guarantee' of the policies end value.

So, to be honest I cannot answer this question honestly, no more than the Governor of the Bank of England could have predicted the recession that we have recently endured.

I mentioned above that one of my partners has experienced continual growth in the area he has identified.

My opinion is this: that all the ingredients that were present in the mid 2000's still exist: Immigration, divorce, the shortage of local authority housing, and the continual increase in population (did you know that there are 700,000 new babies born in the UK every year).

This means that there will always be a demand for housing, the key ingredient that is (temporarily) missing is demand, through the lack of confidence in the market and available funds.

Once confidence returns and the banks make it easier to borrow money, and people see that there is marked increase across the country the housing market will invigorate. I believe it will take another 5 years or so. That suits me just fine, I'll look to invest here and now in the trough, and wait till the market rises.

CHAPTER 9

Buy To Let Finance and Legal Services

Chapter 9. Buy To Let Finance and Legal Services

In order to carry out your purchase you will need the services of a Mortgage Broker and a Solicitor or Conveyancer.

The Mortgage Broker

The mortgage broker, a Financial specialist, will be someone regulated by the FCA - Financial Conduct Authority. In the BTL business you need to have a broker who is 'switched on', someone who is in tune with what you as a property investor needs. They should be mainly approachable and have regular business with the main lenders with favourable rates and quick turn-around times. Some Mortgage brokers tend to deal in the 'domestic' residential mortgage business, you need someone who specialises in the BTL business.

By attending my Master Class and network meetings you will be introduced to the right people who know what your needs are as a property investor.

Your broker will charge you a fee for his services and he receives a small commission from the mortgage lender after completion.

When you apply for a BTL mortgage the broker will need Proof of your Identity by way of a Passport or Driving license, they will hold your details on their file so you don't need to provide this every time you apply for a mortgage.

When you make an application it can all be done over the phone and the application or valuation fee of between £180 and £365 (depending on the lender) can be paid by Debit or Credit Card.

The Solicitor or Conveyancer

As with the Broker, the solicitor you use for your BTL purchase should be one that specialises in these type of conveyances. You wouldn't get your family solicitor who deals with domestic issues to do this work for you.

Over the years I have used one or two solicitors as when you are buying many properties in a year you just want to give them the Instruction, the brief details of the property and the purchase price and leave them to it.

The estate agent that you purchased through will issue a 'memorandum of agreement' to both parties' solicitors which will contain all the relevant information.

As a one-time exercise you will need to provide your ID (this is for money laundering regulations). Once the solicitor receives your instructions he will write to you confirming the details and their fees. They will request that you pay an 'on account' payment of £250 or so to cover the costs they incur when applying to the Local Authorities for searches.

Your solicitor will write to your seller's solicitor to confirm they are instructed and request a copy of the draft contract and any other details, such as the property's title and the standard forms. Once received, the solicitor will examine the draft contract and supporting documents and raise enquiries with the seller's solicitor. You will be expected to go through the forms the seller has completed and let the solicitor know if you have any queries or concerns. In particular you will want to double check the tenure of the property: is it leasehold or freehold? If leasehold, leases below 80 years are a problem, can be costly to extend and you need to have owned the property for 2 years before you are eligible to do so. Leases under 60 years are best avoided.

The solicitor will obtain property searches. There are things you may not know about the property just from viewing it with estate agents or even getting a survey. The conveyancer will do a set of legal and environmental searches to ensure there are no other factors you should be aware that may adversely affect the property, this can cost between £70 and £400 depending on the area and usually takes 1-2 weeks, but can take up to 6 weeks, The Environmental search from the Environmental Agency will show whether plots used to be a landfill site or there are flooding issues nearby. They will

Check the 'title register' and 'title plan' at the Land Registry which are the legal documents proving the seller's ownership. The title register check costs £8 and the title plan check costs £4. Both are legally required to sell. Be careful here, the solicitor will not know the property or will not have seen it, you must ensure that the title plan represents what you are buying, make sure when you view the property, that you check the boundary positions and that they accord with the title plan.

You will receive Water Authority searches showing the water mains and if any public drains are on the property. The water authority search will cost between £50 and £75. Now and again you may be advised of a Chancel repair search, to ensure there are no potential leftover medieval liabilities on the property to help pay for church repairs. This is crops up now and again and costs £18. However, you may decide to take out Chancel repair insurance instead for £20 or so. The laws around Chancel repair changed in October 2013 so now the onus is on the Church to establish and lodge liability with the Land Registry. Your solicitor will advise in any case.

If you buying with a mortgage you will need to get this in place. This will include ensuring you have the financing available for a deposit, usually 25%. Your solicitor will receive a copy of the offer and go through the conditions. Before exchange of contracts can take place your lender will require you to get Buildings Insurance for the property. You are responsible for the property as soon as contracts have been exchanged so it is in your interests to do so.

Your solicitor will receive the draft contract from the seller's solicitor. Before asking you to sign the contract, your solicitor will need to ensure that all enquiries have been returned and are satisfactory and that fixtures and fittings included in the purchase are what you expected. They will check with you and propose a completion date, which is usually 4 to 12 weeks after exchange of contracts.

A payment of usually 10% (negotiable) of the value of the purchase will be requested from you for the exchange and you must transfer the funds into your solicitor's account so that it is cleared in time for an exchange. (Cash is not allowed). However, even if you agree to pay less than 10% you are still liable for 10% of the value of the property if you later pull out of the agreement. Therefore if you pay a 5% payment and pull out of buying the property you will not only lose your money but also legally owe an additional 5% of the value of the property

Your solicitor will agree and arrange with the seller's solicitor to exchange contracts for you. This is usually done by both solicitors/ conveyancers reading out the contracts over the phone (which is recorded) to make sure the contracts are identical, and then immediately sending them to one another in the post. If you are in a chain your solicitor/conveyancer will do the same thing, but will only release it if the other people in the chain are all happy to go ahead. This means if one person pulls out or delays, then everyone in the chain gets held up.

Once you have exchanged contracts you will be in a legally binding contract to buy the property with a fixed date for moving. This means that if you do not complete the purchase, you will lose your deposit and owe the seller more if the deposit was less than 10% and the seller has to sell to you, they can not for example decide to accept a higher offer from someone else.

Once contracts are exchanged your solicitor will lodge an interest in the property which will mean that the deeds to the property are frozen for 30 working days to allow you to pay the seller and lodge your application to the Land Registry to transfer the deeds into your name.

Shortly after you should receive a 'completion statement' showing the final figure to pay, including their fee which will need to be cleared into your solicitors bank account at least one day before completion. Completion is normally set around midday on the specified date although in practice takes place when the seller's solicitor confirms that they have received all the money that is due. Once this happens the seller should drop the keys at the estate agents for your collection, you should get a call around 3-4pm saying that the keys are available to you. When collecting the keys, the agents will ask you to sign for them.

The solicitor will register your interest and the details of the lender with the Land Registry, and after a few weeks you should receive the title documents from the solicitor which will now show your names on the Land Registry Title.

As with the broker, I will be able to recommend suitable solicitors to use. The fees for their conveyance will be between £400 and £600 plus the expenses referred to.

Mike's tip!

When you receive the Title Plan from the solicitor make sure that you check the plan 'edged in Red' and that what is shown is what you are actually buying. Getting this wrong can lead to lengthy and costly boundary disputes, which will severely affect your project.

The Lenders

Of course little happens in your early stages of building a property portfolio without having to borrow money.

Buy to Let Mortgages are loans where the money is secured against the property, 'The Security', and the Rental Income. As these mortgages are not residential they do not rely on your personal income. They are based on the rental income of the property.

As mentioned the amount that you can borrow is typically 75% of the value of the property that you are buying, however they impose a limit on what they will lend relative to the rental income of 125%. -called a multiplier.

For example if the repayment is £400 the rent must be £500. 400 x 1.25 = 500

This is to ensure that there is sufficient 'cover' over the rent, which in a way is a safety net for you.

A little research will find that there are various 'mortgage products' on the market at any one time; the companies constantly change the deals that they have available depending on the level of funding available to them.

The main 3 products are, Fixed rate, Trackers and Standard Variable.

Each product will have application fees and vary depending on the product, these fees which are usually added to the loan vary from fixed fees of £999 to £1999 or are % of the loan, typically 2.5-3%. In addition there will be the Valuation fee. The valuation fee is non-refundable, but the application fee is only charged when you accept the mortgage.

Fixed rate mortgages are as you would imagine: the interest rate is fixed for a given period, these can be between 2 and 5 years, after which they change to a rate specified which can be around 1.75% over base. I rarely fix a rate for more than 2 years.

Tracker mortgages are those which 'track' or follow the Bank of England base rate, for example 1.5% over base. So as the recent BOE base rate is 0.5% your rate will be 2% if the BOE rate goes up by 0.5% so will your mortgage, at the end of the contract period the interest will change to a specified rate similar to the above.

Standard variable mortgages are those that are offered at a given rate set by the lender, say 4.5%, and if the lender rate changes either up or down as a result of the BOE base rate change, so will your mortgage.

Many Professional Property Investors arrange 'Interest Only' mortgages, the reasons for this are two-fold. They see that asset as a vehicle, they never want to 'own' it outright as it's a cash cow. As the value of the property rises they will re-mortgage and keep pulling money out of it. This re-mortgaged money is not taxable, so it can be used as you see fit, to re-invest, go on holiday, buy a new car etc.

Some investors do want to see their level of gearing reduced over the period of the mortgage so some will pay down the debt by using profits from other income streams, like the money they make from selling a refurbishment.

As expected with an `Interest Only' mortgage you pay just the interest on the loan, this keeps the payment to a minimum in order to maximize profit. With "Repayment' mortgages you pay both interest and capital. After 25 years you will have paid off the loan, but as the years go by the amount of interest reduces. As you are only able to offset Interest against tax your tax bill increases.

Mike's top tip!

Make yourself seen to be investable by the lenders, build a good credit file, check your credit file regularly. Close any credit card accounts you don't need. Make sure you are on the Electoral Register.

CHAPTER 10

Tenancy Agreements, Management, Tenants and Deposits

Chapter 10. Tenancy Agreements, Management, Tenants and Deposits

Tenancy Agreements.

All tenants by law and in accordance with the Housing Act 1988 must have a Tenancy Agreement known as an 'Assured Shorthold Tenancy', this agreement allows the tenant to occupy the house and the landlord to charge a market rent.

The AST contains the 'rules' of the tenancy, many tenancy agreement templates are available on the Internet or from various publications. The rules are generally as follows:

1. The Address of the rental property
2. The Start and end date of the tenancy
3. The rent payable and the frequency
4. The do's and don'ts e.g.. No animals, no decoration, etc.
5. The bond or deposit required (usually equal to 1 month's rent)

An AST is usually issued for 6 months. I issue 6 months agreements, this gives both me and the tenant the chance to review the situation after 6 months. If I and the tenant wish to continue the arrangement I can issue a new 6 month or 1 year tenancy. Some Landlords do not issue a new tenancy agreement after the expiry of the first, this does not mean that the tenant or you have lost any rights under the original agreement. The tenancy then becomes what is known as a 'periodic tenancy', but the rules under the original tenancy still apply.

All AST's state a requirement that the tenant pays a bond or deposit, but this is not compulsory, and some landlords with less than attractive or desirable property often waive this requirement. However, if a bond is paid it must be 'secured' or deposited in a registered scheme. (see the TDS section later) This is to protect the bond on behalf of the tenant as in the past many landlords have simply not returned the bond to the tenant or the tenant has difficulty in getting it back. There are strict rules to protecting a bond and the punishment to the landlord if the matter goes to court is expensive.

Management.

Once you have prepared your property for a tenant, and have received enquiries, I recommend you ask them a series of questions.

Are they currently renting? Where? Why are they looking to rent your property? How old are they? And most crucially ask them to explain their circumstances...this makes for interesting reading. You will be surprised what you will read.

Unfortunately, a female advising you that they have just split up, and going through an acrimonious divorce from a violent partner may well sound heart breaking, but often the desperation will lead the prospective tenant to pour their hearts out. However you are not a social worker and can not help them with their domestic issue. Your concern is to ensure that your property is going to be looked after and not become the location where a potential 'Bomb' is going to go off.

Once you have made a shortlist of the potential tenants, arrange to a viewing at the house, try and arrange 2-4 over an hour or so, 1.00, 1.20 and 1.40 etc. this allows you to do your viewing in one 'hit' you can see all potential tenants instead of doing 3 or 4 trips to the property at various times of the day.

Advise them politely that you will be interviewing all applicants and will give the matter your consideration overnight. Some applicants will expect you to agree there and then, by saying to you that they will take it and they have the money with them. Don't fall for this, if someone is in that much of a rush...what are they rushing from?

Take all the applicants contact details and confirm that you will let them know the next day. After all you want to be confident that your prospective tenant is serious and you feel that you can trust them with your investment.

If your house is in good order and attractive you will find yourself in a dilemma where you will wish you had 3 houses available, as they will all want it. Unfortunately you will only be able to offer it to one person or family.

Once you have decided who you are going to let the house to, let the others know by phone or email, not by text, by thanking them for their time, but you have decided to offer it to the another person of family for no other reason than that is who you felt you could work with.

Once you have agreed the terms of the tenancy and the commencement date, you should prepare an inventory of the condition of the house and have them sign it as they move in. You should also advise them of the utility suppliers and take meter reading for Gas Electricity and Water.

Provide them with your contact details and the details of your plumber or electrician in cases of emergency. Advise your plumber or electrician that if they get a call out that they should clear it with you first. Assess the problem and advise accordingly. If the matter can wait until the morning or Monday this will avoid a potentially unnecessary call out fee.

DSS/LHA Tenants

If you have agreed to take on a tenant that is claiming LHA -Local Housing Allowance, you need to get them to provide you with a letter from the Benefits section at the Local Authority confirming what benefit they are able to claim. Each local Authority in England and Wales have their own level of benefits these can be found at here: lha-direct.voa.gov.uk/search.aspx

You can expect the Local Authority to pay between £48-90 per week for your tenant; if the rent that you are charging per week is more your tenant will have to find the difference, known as the 'top-up'. Housing benefit is usually paid 4 weekly in arrears. You will have initially requested a bond and an advance rent in your AST, this often poses a problem for a tenant on benefits as they are sometimes unable to get a sum in the region of £800-900 together. The strictness of how you deal with this is up to you, but from my experience if someone can not pay a bond and doesn't, they have nothing to lose when they leave and often they leave your property in a mess.

What irritates me here, is that well-meaning landlords such as myself have to comply with laws set down by parliament to protect the tenants, however there is absolutely nothing to protect the landlord against a tenant trashing the house prior to leaving. You may have a bond that is relative to 1 month's rent, but that will not go anywhere near the cost of making good the property for the next tenant. In the past I must admit I have been far too easy going and not doing as I now preach, take a cash bond, not a paper bond or a bond certificate issued by the council or a bond board. When the tenant has little or no 'cash' invested in the house, they simply walk away and leave a mess and leave anything that they can not carry, old clothes, furniture, knackered beds and sofas I've had it all. I also insist on a Guarantor, someone who is employed and a homeowner. I realise that it seems pretty obvious to have these things in place, but I ran my own property portfolio up until the middle of 2013, that was over 35 houses and knew every tenant.

My leniency has cost me dearly over the years, as mentioned I would give someone a break, let them into a house, listen to their story about this and that and how they really need somewhere to live, only for them to up and leave when it suits them, usually without informing me. Often the first I would know about it would be either a letter from the Council tax section advising me as the property is empty it is exempt for 6 months, or a letter from the Housing benefit section, saying that 'the benefit has stopped because the tenant has vacated the property'.

Some DSS tenants will ask you if they can pay a bond to you every 2 to 4 weeks after they move in, as your experience grows you will learn how to deal with this, but at this early stage I would not recommend that you do this. Unfortunately a tenant's desire to move into your nicely prepared house will make them say whatever they need to get through the door, once through the urgency wanes and the excuses flow as to why they can't pay you this week or the next.

However, having said that, some of the best tenant that I have are DSS tenants particularly the over 35's Male or Female. The most trouble I have had, trouble by way of arrears and damage to houses has generally been from younger people, some just don't have the sense of responsibility. I have agreed to let houses to young females with children and at first they try and get the house as they want, but all too often they meet a young man and the parties start, there are complaints from neighbours, often domestic violence and the whole situation falls apart. The rent falls into arrears, because they are only in receipt of other allowances, their ability to catch up is slim. All too often after they have gone the door mat is flooded with letters from debt collectors, from the phone companies, catalogues, Betterware and of course the utility companies, you name it. And for the next few months the new tenant is plagued by debt collectors.

The stories that I could tell you would be enough to fill a book in itself, I would be happy to share these with you at one of our Network meetings or during our One to One mentoring sessions.

As of 2013, my wife and I set up a letting agency called SM Property Rentals in the town where the bulk of the properties are, where we offer a letting service to other landlords based on our values and quality of property. I now have very little to do with the day to day running of the properties and tenants - after all it's not what I'm best at, and I can concentrate more on sourcing new properties for us to buy to rent, to refurbish and flip or to offer to other landlords.

Mike's tip!

When dealing with all tenants ensure that they pay a deposit and have a guarantor, being too easy going in the past has cost me dearly.

Private Tenants

The term Private tenants tends to be used where they are not DSS tenants. As with any tenant the tenancy agreement and the 'Check in' procedure remains the same.

Private tenants are usually people who are working and will come to you confirming that they have a bond and a month's rent in advance, in accordance with the AST they will make monthly advance payments of the rent throughout the duration of the agreement.

Without being disrespectful to DSS tenants, the Private tenant will be a little more responsible and appreciative of your property and your position as a landlord.

Eviction Process

Unfortunately, there will come a time when you need to evict a tenant. Since I have been letting property I have had to issue eviction notices on many occasions, fortunately I have never needed to go to court and involve bailiffs. Maybe this is because I live locally to my houses, maybe because I have made a solid argument to my tenants that I'm not prepared to subsidise them anymore. Ensuring that I write to tenants the moment that I become aware that they have fallen into arrears or there is a reason that I feel that I want them to leave is vitally important.

Regretfully, the most problems I have had have been with the younger benefit tenants, I have given many a chance, provided them with a nice house only for them to abuse the property, not pay the utility bills and fall into arrears and run up huge debts. It never fails to surprise me that after they have left the number of Red letters that come through door weeks after they have left, not to mention the regular from debt collectors. The amount of debt out there with phone companies, Utility companies, catalogues to name a few must be massive.

When these tenants run up massive debts the pattern is common, and the only way is for them to up sticks and run, and they don't bother cleaning the house before they go either. The take much of what they can carry and what is valuable to them, the rest they leave for you.

So, how do you go about asking someone to leave? Well as mentioned you need to write to them as above stating that they are in arrears and be sure to include a schedule of their payments. Hopefully you will get a response, invariably by text, regretfully they will rarely apologise.

The two responses I usually receive are: 'I haven't got any money' or 'I'll go to the bank by the end of the week to put some in, how much do I owe you'?

There is a procedure that you should keep to when looking to evict someone, firstly do not harass them; simply calling at the house every few days and sending regular texts asking them to address the problem can be seen as harassment! The last thing I will do is give them ammunition to use against me. Write to them first bringing the matter to their attention and ask them to make payment within 7 days. If they do make an effort and start to make payments and enter into dialogue with me about setting up a structure of regular payment I will go with them and give them a chance.

No matter how frustrated you are, and believe me the audacity of some tenants is amazing, do not, turn the electricity or gas off, change the locks or refuse to carry out repairs as this is illegal. This is the one that gets me, the tenants 6 weeks in arrears avoids me for weeks and then sends a text saying that the boilers stopped working, and casually asks if I can send the plumber round.

If the tenants do not make an effort, I will write to them after 7 days advising them that I intend taking court proceeding against them by issuing a county court summons. Unfortunately 'some' tenants especially the LHA tenants may well already have CCJ's so another one will make little difference to them. This is where it is important when you select your tenants you need to ensure you have a process in place; in all honesty in the past I didn't, and whilst I didn't let just anyone, rent from me, if I had a house and it was not renting for a while I would tend to reduce the criteria somewhat, and believe me this is a mistake, trust me.

I will contact them by text, I won't beat about the bush, I will tell them that I'm not happy, that I am disappointed that they are avoiding me and that this can't go on indefinitely. After a period of about 4 weeks, I won't be surprised to go by the house one day and see that it is empty.

Section 21 (a) and (b)

As mentioned though, there is a process that you must adhere to and prescribed notices. If you want to ask someone to leave at the end of the tenancy you must issue a Section 21 Notice (b) and this notice must be issued before the end of the fourth month, asking the tenant to leave at the end of the tenancy. If the tenancy has gone 'periodic' which means that they are still living at the property after the initial 6 months and you have not issued another tenancy agreement, it is known as a periodic tenancy; if you want them to leave during this period you must issue a Section 21 Notice (a), again giving them 2 months' notice to leave.

What is critical in both cases is that you must issue and they must receive the notices before the anniversary date of their tenancy. So for example if their tenancy commenced on the 1st of January in the case of a section 21b you must issue the notice before the 30th April, In order to end their tenancy on the 30th June.

In the case of periodic tenancy and you want them to leave by the 30th November, you must issue Section 21a by 30th September. Failure to get this right and the tenant decides not to take notice of your 'notice', you will have to apply to the court for the court to issue a possession order, if during the court hearing the tenant or indeed the Judge sees that you have not issued the notice in the correct manner and on the correct date, he will throw your claim out of court and you will have to start the process again. If you have done it all correctly that the court should grant a Possession order and it will require the tenant to vacate by a specific date, which 'can' be within 2 months!

The Notice requiring Possession under Section 21 does not end the tenancy, but gives you the Absolute right to apply for and obtain an order for possession when the notice expires.

There is another aspect of common error made by people when completing a section 21 and that is to insert a date that the notice period ends, and if this is seen as being incorrect by the court, your claim will be thrown out. i.e. dismissed because of a technicality.

Notice N5B

However, there is also what is known as 'accelerated possession'; if you have correctly given the requisite notice to your tenant asking them to leave at the end of the tenancy and they fail to do so, you can claim for possession using a form N5B. You will need to send the court the name and address of your tenant, the address of the property, the dates of the tenancy agreement and the date you served your notice and when the notice period ended. The court will base its decision on the written evidence provided by you and your tenant if they respond. In the event all is on order the court will issue a possession order and will normally take effect between 2 and 4 weeks after the decision. If the tenant claims that this will cause them exceptional hardship, the court may delay the order for up to 6 weeks before they must leave.

If the tenant doesn't leave the house by the date given in an outright possession order, you can ask the court for a 'warrant for possession'. If the court gives a warrant, your tenant will be sent an eviction notice that gives a date when they must leave the house.

If they don't go, bailiffs can evict them. The costs of doing this will be added to the money order. As mentioned in the 25 years I have been a landlord I have never needed to take such action, so don't let it frighten you off.

Court Costs-Possession orders with a money judgment

A judge can add a money judgment to any of the possession orders. This means your tenant will owe a specific amount of money, usually made up of:

- Rent arrears
- Court fees
- Your legal costs
- Bailiff costs

Section 8

A section 8 notice is used where the Landlord wants to evict the tenant for reasons other than a Section 21, there are a number of reasons and these are termed as 'Grounds'. Some Grounds require that the court must issue a Possession Order, for others the court has discretion over.

Once the Section 8 notice has been filled out, it must be sent to all of the tenants living at the address. It is often recommended that the landlord sends it via first class post and at a post office where proof of postage can be obtained. Don't send it recorded delivery as the tenants will often not accept to sign for it and if they don't it will be returned to the post office, and of course they will not be bothered to go and get it.

It is usually customary to allow a minimum of three working days for the notice to arrive at the address of the tenant. The Section 8 notice expires two weeks or two months after this date, depending on the grounds being cited. It is only once the Section 8 notice has expired, and the issue has not been resolved, that the landlord can apply for a possession order from the court.

Once the Section 8 notice has been served, the landlord can apply to the court for a hearing to get a **Possession Order** using the forms N119 and N5 and by paying the court fees.

The landlord is then given a date to attend court, the first hearing, and must attend on this date. If the tenant has not filed a Defence or does not attend court to challenge the claim, the court may make a possession order at the first hearing. If the tenant does defend the claim, the court will issue directions at the First Hearing and adjourn the claim until a further hearing when the case will be heard in full. If the possession order is granted then it takes effect 14 days after it has been issued, although in some cases this may be extended to six weeks where it is deemed that the tenant will face serious hardship as a result of the repossession.

Grounds for Eviction

When the Section 8 notice is served, the landlord must base the decision to apply for a possession order on one or more of 17 grounds. The court will then decide whether to grant a possession order based on these grounds.

The amount of notice that must be given to the tenant differs depending on the grounds. For grounds 1, 2, 5, 6, 7, 9 and 16, two months' notice or more must be given. For grounds 3, 4, 8, 10, 11, 12, 13, 15 and 17, two weeks' notice is required. In the case of ground 14A, proceedings can be started immediately after serving the notice.

Grounds 1 to 8 are Mandatory, meaning if the landlord can prove to the court that they apply then the court must grant the possession order. The other grounds are all discretionary.

Ground 1

Used when the landlord wants to live in the property as a permanent home. It is only permitted when the landlord has already lived in it as their main home or they, or their spouse require it to live in as his or her main home. Evidence of this may be required together with evidence that the landlord intends to, or must, leave their current home.

Ground 2

Used when the property is subject to a mortgage which existed before the start of the tenancy and the landlord wants to possess the property.

Ground 3

Used when the tenancy is for a period of a maximum of eight months and the property was occupied as a holiday let within the period of twelve months prior to the start of the tenancy. Written notice must be given before or at the start of the tenancy that possession might be recovered based on this ground.

Ground 4

Used when the tenancy is for a period of no more than 12 months and the property belongs to an educational institution. Written notice must be given before or at the start of the tenancy that possession might be recovered based on this ground.

Ground 5

Used when the property is being used by a minister of religion and is required for another minister. Written notice must be given before or at the start of the tenancy that possession might be recovered based on this ground.

Ground 6

Used when the landlord wants to reconstruct, demolish or carry out works on part or all of the property which cannot go ahead with the tenant there, perhaps because the tenant will not allow access. If this ground is used, the landlord has to pay reasonable removal costs.

Ground 7

Used when the previous tenant has deceased and the tenancy has passed to a new tenant but the new tenant does not have the right to carry on with the tenancy. Proceedings must be brought within 12 months following the death of the tenant, or within 12 months of the landlord becoming aware of the death of the tenant.

Ground 8

Used when the rent is still in arrears on the date that the Section 8 notice is served and on the date of the hearing. Where rent is due weekly or fortnightly, at least 8 weeks' rent must be in arrears. Where rent is due monthly, at least two months' rent must be in arrears. Where rent is due quarterly, at least a quarter's rent must be in arrears by more than three months. Where rent is due yearly, at least three months' rent must be in arrears by more than three months.

Ground 9

This ground states that alternative accommodation will be available for the tenant in the case that the possession order is made and that the landlord has to pay reasonable removal expenses.

Ground 10

Used when any amount of rent is due on the date that the Section 8 notice is served and is still due on the date that proceedings begin.

Ground 11

Used when the tenant has failed on a regular basis to pay the rent. Rent does not have to be in arrears on the date that the Section 8 notice is served.

Ground 12

Used when there has been a breach of any term of the tenancy agreement.

Ground 13

Used when the property has been neglected by the tenant or someone living in the property with the tenant who the tenant has not removed and as a result the condition of the property has deteriorated.

Ground 14

Used when the tenant has caused problems with neighbours, visitors or anyone else, has used the property for illegal or immoral purposes and received a conviction for this, or has received a conviction for an indictable offence in or near the property.

Ground 14a

Used when the property is occupied by a couple and one member of the couple has left due to violence or threats from the other partner towards the partner who has left or a member of their family who was residing in the property. This ground only applies to property which is owned by a charitable housing trust or registered social landlord.

Ground 15

Used when the furniture in the property has been treated badly by the tenant or by someone residing in the property who the tenant has not removed.

Ground 16

Used when the tenant was employed by the landlord of the property and has now left the landlord's employment.

Ground 17

Used when the landlord gave permission for the tenancy based on a false statement which was made knowingly by the tenant.

Tenancy Deposit Scheme

What is it?

It is common for landlords to take a dilapidation deposit from a tenant at the start of the tenancy. The deposit acts as a safeguard should the tenant cause any damage to the property. Some unscrupulous landlords are either very slow to return deposits at the end of the tenancy or make unfair deductions. The purpose of the regulations is to ensure good practice in this area, and try to keep disputes between landlords and tenants out of the courts by encouraging alternative dispute resolution.

The tenant pays over the deposit (commonly one month's rent) in the usual way when the tenancy agreement is signed. The landlord or letting agency has 30 days from receipt of the deposit to provide the tenant with details of the scheme that they are using (known as the prescribed information). If there is no dispute at the end of the tenancy the deposit will be returned to the two parties as agreed. If a dispute has arisen then the parties will be invited to make use of the alternative dispute resolution process that is provided free within the scheme. Should the parties opt for alternative dispute resolution they will be bound by its decision with no redress to the courts.

There are two types of scheme: insurance backed and custodial. Under insurance backed schemes the landlord or letting agency pays a premium to the scheme but retains the deposit. With custodial schemes the deposit is transferred to the scheme within the 30 day timescale and held in escrow.

Penalties to Landlord

If a landlord or letting agent does not both protect a tenant's deposit and provide the tenant with the prescribed information within 30 days then they have no right to regain possession of the property under a Section 21 notice, unless the deposit is first repaid.

If the tenant applies to court for the deposit to be protected or because it was not returned and it is shown the landlord was not compliant with the scheme, then the court must order the landlord to pay the tenant three times the deposit amount within 14 days.

Prescribed Information

The following is prescribed information for the purposes of section 213 of the Housing Act 2004 ("the Act")—

- the name, address and contact details of the scheme administrator
- any information supplied by the scheme administrator to the landlord which explains the relevant sections the Act
- the amount in respect of a deposit may be paid or repaid
- the procedures that apply under the scheme where either the landlord or the tenant is not contactable at the end of the tenancy
- the facilities available to resolve a dispute relating to the deposit

- the full details of the tenancy

For the details of the full information, the scheme administrators should provide you with the full information, and you should ensure that this information is given to the tenant.

Court Cases

Ayannuga v Swindells

In the case of Ayannuga v Swindells, the landlord failed to provide details of the procedures to be followed in certain events. Details of the Tenancy Deposit Scheme had been provided, but the landlord omitted to provide all the additional information, the prescribed information. The fine was three times the deposit, but the landlord also forfeited the original deposit, so in reality it is four times.

All residential landlords and letting agents need to take note of the important decision in this case and make sure that they provide all the necessary prescribed information, ideally well within the 30 days allowed.'

Superstrike vs. Rodrigues

The Court of Appeal case of Superstrike vs. Rodrigues concerns an assured shorthold tenancy that was created in January 2007 prior to the introduction of mandatory tenancy deposit protection on 6 April 2007. The tenancy continued on a statutory periodic basis from January 2008 and the deposit remained unprotected. In 2011 a Section 21 notice was served to end the tenancy.

The Court of Appeal has ruled that when the tenancy continued on a statutory periodic basis in 2008 a new tenancy was made and a new deposit was deemed to have been received, and therefore fell under the requirements of tenancy deposit protection legislation. Having not met those requirements (to protect the deposit and serve Prescribed Information (PI), including serving the scheme leaflet, or equivalent) the landlord was not entitled to serve a s21 notice.

CHAPTER 11

Tax issues: Responsibilities, Income Tax, and Tax Relief

Chapter 11. Tax issues: Responsibilities, Income Tax, and Tax Relief

This section is for general guidance and does not intend to be exhaustive. As you will be receiving income from your buy-to-let property you are advised to employ an Accountant who will prepare your tax return and submit them to HMRC. Failure to submit accurate accounts can lead to fines. I have always used a Chartered Certified Accountant and would recommend that you do so instead of a book keeper or a friend of a friend.

Your rental income is known as 'un-earned' income, you do not need to be a company or an officially registered business to make money from buy to let property. The money you receive less legitimate expenses is taxable.

Typical legitimate expenses are, the Interest on your loan, expenses incurred while running your portfolio, e.g. Some fuel costs and the costs of a vehicle that you need in order to run the 'business'. The use of a room in your house or office inc heat and light from which you operate your business and the costs of maintaining your rental property. e.g. Plumber call out and repairs etc.

You can also claim the cost of the repairs to your property, but not the cost of any improvements. Other allowable costs are professional fees and advertising.

If you are employed on a PAYE basis you will pay your tax through your employer and therefore will pay tax on all the profits from your BTL property or properties. If you are self-employed, your accountant will complete your self-assessment tax return using the figures that you provide through the running of your business and will treat the income from your properties separately. Your accountant cannot off-set losses from one business to your profitable BTL income, unfortunately. However, you can carry losses forward and set them off against profit you make in subsequent years.

There is an HMRC allowance known as 'Rent a room' the details of which can be found on the HMRC website under ref PIM4001, this allowance basically allows you to receive payments of up to £4250 per year for renting a room out in your own home tax free. You 'may' want to include this amount when preparing your year-end accounts.

CHAPTER 12

Splitting Titles to Increase values

Chapter 12. Splitting Titles to Increase values

Some of you may be aware of the concept of taking a building that is made up of individual units, flats for example that are under a single title and then creating multiple titles i.e. giving each flat its own title, which in turn allows you to secure a mortgage on the individual unit. By doing this, often the sum total value of the individual titles is more than the value of the units when under a single title.

There are a number of different building types and ways to do this but again, for ease of explanation I will give you an example of such a scheme that I did in 2007, from which you will get a basic understanding of the practice.

In the Spring of 2007, I had arranged to have a coffee with my friend and mentor Billy and during the conversation he mentioned that he was selling what we referred to as Nichol St; I knew he was breaking away from one of his partners and this building was jointly owned. Basically it was a Car Repair Garage, second hand furniture shop and small upholstery workshop, and above it all were 4 flats, 2, 2 Bedroom and 2, 1 Bedroom. He advised that he had instructed a local commercial agent to put it on the market for £525,000.

He had owned the building for over 30 years, the main unit the garage was leased to a guy who was 7 years into his second 15 year lease, the furniture shop were on an easy in/easy out agreement as was the upholsterer. The flats were all let on AST's and the whole building was bringing £45,000 per year. He suggested that it would a great property to add to my portfolio. I really liked the idea of owning such a property, I had built up a solid portfolio of individual units, I felt it was time to take on something a little more substantial.

I called my bank manager, who was also Billy's manager and asked him would he lend me the money to buy it, he knew Billy was selling it as it had been funded through him, he agreed and confirmed that he would lend me 70%. This meant that I would have to find £157,500 plus fees. I was currently in the middle of refurbishing the Trullo in Italy and needed to find some more money from the portfolio. I sat down and scrutinised all the properties looking to see where I could re-mortgage and pull money from.

As I saw it I could only immediately raise £75,000 half of what I needed, I was a little deflated, I really liked this idea of having Nichol St, but perhaps it wasn't to be.

I called the bank manager and explained my position, and he advised that the money was there if I needed it. I tried to put it out of my mind, but I just couldn't let it go. When I look back over the things that I have done, it seems that I have more than often got what I wanted, is this coincidence? I think not, recently talking to Kevin Green we discussed the 'Power of Intention' and I now truly believe it to be a formidable force.

A number of months went by and I couldn't quite get the property out of my head, there had to be a way of buying it. I met with Billy again for a coffee, Nichol St came up in conversation again and Billy said that he hadn't had much interest in it and was prepared to sell it to me for £500,000 and re- affirmed that it would be a great addition to the portfolio.

For the next few days I reviewed my position and by chance during conversation with my solicitor (who was also Billy's) Nichol St came up; he said that he had been talking to Billy about it as he had opened a file in readiness for its sale, he mentioned that the bank had recently valued the building and valued the commercial element, the ground floor at £350,000, this was a 'eureka' moment, if the ground floor was valued at £350,000 and I was looking to buying for £500,000 that meant that the theoretical value of the flats was £150,000, 4 flats in the centre of Swansea for £37,500 each? They were surely worth more than that and if I were to get residential mortgages on them at 85% LTV I would reduce the amount of deposit I needed.

I did some research and confirmed that the 1 Bedroom flats were worth £60,000 and the 2 bedroom flats £70,000.

I called the bank manager and discussed the valuation report that he commissioned and asked him if would entertain lending me on the commercial part of the building if I split the title and then got residential funding on the flats - he agreed.

So the figures looked like this

Commercial valuation £350,000 x 70% LTV =	£245,000
2 Bed flats valuation £140,000 x 85% LTV =	£119,000
1 Bed flats valuation £120,000 x 85% LTV =	£102,000
Total funds raised	£466,000

Funds to find £500,000 - £466,000 = **£34,000** plus fees

So, I set about making applications for BTL mortgages on the flats and subsequently received offers on the figures I had included on my applications. The bank manager raised the required loan documents for signing.

The next step was for the solicitor to split the title of the building, I arranged to meet with the solicitor and discuss my plan, he agreed that it was all possible, we would need have plans prepared of each of the flats and the ground floor (no problem there for me) and create 4 leases for the flats and a freehold for the ground floor and 5 separate titles. We would need to create a management company to create a layer between me and the seller. The management company would be needed for the future as if I decided to sell any of the flats the owners would take a share in the company. The management company would be responsible for arranging maintenance of repairs of the whole building.

What was to happen was, the management company would buy the building for £500,000 and I would what is called 'back to back' complete on the purchase of the flats off the management company for the price stipulated by the company which was now £610,000. I would raise funds of £245,000 from the bank and a total of £221,000 from the BTL lender. And I would need to stump up the balance, which was now only £34,000 instead of £157,000. The completions are instantaneous and have to be done by individual solicitors within a practice representing each party.

But there were also the fees to pay, which amounted to £2,500 plus VAT and the bank arrangement fee. Also and finally something I had over looked, Stamp Duty! As I hadn't purchased anything over £125,000 before, Stamp duty was off my radar and Stamp duty on a purchase of £500,000 was 4% another £20,000!

Stamp duty has to be paid via the solicitor on completion so there was no way of delaying this. If the purchase price was under £500,000 then Stamp Duty would be 2% which would equate to £10,000, so I placed a call to Billy and negotiated a further discount to bring the price below £500,000, saving me £10,000.

Clearly, Billy has been more than a mentor to me, a true friend and has helped me many times, I in turn have made sure when in need I have been there for him, not only providing personal support but professional.

As you travel on your property investment journey, you will learn that you do not only make money when buying, refurbishing, renting and selling property, but when you mix with experienced property professionals and by having a mentor, their experience will rub off on you and you will learn of ways of maximising profits.

CHAPTER 13

New Build - Self Builds

Chapter 13. New Build - Self Builds

Over the last couple of years I have been offered a number of small plots, typically to build semi-detached houses, but in all honesty in the area where I invest the cost of the plots even at £20,000 each that's £40,000 for a pair, but because of the ever increasing requirements of insulation standards and the need to incorporate renewable energy systems like, solar panels, air source heat pumps or ground source heat pumps to comply with what is known as 'Code for sustainable development' the cost of a small new build has become from a developers point of view uneconomical and the profits are slim.

However, If you were able to access to sufficient funds and did feel a new build project was for you it can provide an excellent start to build a cash pot for your property portfolio, but doing it one by one will be slow going.

Be aware, that there is a great tax break when it comes to new builds as individuals known as 'Private Resident Relief', and that is, you are allowed to own two homes at any one time and are able to sell one with no Capital gains tax to pay, so, for example, you own your own home, you build a new one and move in, then sell the first one. There is no tax to pay on the first; if you build another whilst living in the second house, and then move in to the third house, selling the second, there is no tax to pay!

However, if you do this prolifically, the tax man 'may' claim that you are acting as a 'developer' so having a good accountant and keeping him fully informed will help you greatly. In all honesty I have not known this to actually happen though.

Note that the tax relief is for each individual, so if you register the first house in your name and second in your wife's or husband's name, then you get two bites of the cherry. The first build is yours the second your partners, the third yours, the forth your partners and so on. Each time your sell 'your home' it is tax free! Sound good?

Undertaking a new build project can be exciting, from locating and purchasing the plot, instructing your Architectural designer, seeing your ideas begin to take shape in the form of foundations, external walls, the roof and ultimately being able to walk around the house, going up the stairs and looking out of the windows and taking in a view that has never been seen from that position before. I really enjoy building new houses. They are quite easy to do, unfortunately, the availability of funds for new build for developers has diminished somewhat over the years, also because of the costs of the renewables, it is quicker to buy a terraced house, refurbish it and get it back on the market for sale.

But as individuals making a start, being able to taking advantage of the PPR, I would certainly consider it.

To give you an idea of the procedure let's run through a scenario that I have done a number of times. Again though as with any property purchase you need to run the numbers, and your proposed location will have a massive influence.

When people ask me is there a simple calculation for working out new build, unfortunately there is not. Some people talk in terms of the plot and that it should be should be 30% of the end value and the build should be 30-40% leaving £30-40% profit, but it doesn't work out that way. The cost of plots and the labour costs vary greatly across the country, as does the potential end value of the property.

In addition, new builds are zero VAT rated, so the VAT on all your costs (except professional fees and some luxury items) re-claimable at the end of the project. Once the build has been signed off by the Building Control officer you must send all your receipts together with your VAT claim form, Planning Approval and Completion Certificate to the VAT office. You will receive all the documents back after approximately six weeks and your bank account will be credited. Please refer to guidance notes VAT431NB

A great way to start finding yourself a plot that will accommodate a pair of semi-detached houses, is if you are able to locate a large garden by searching Google maps and Ordnance Survey maps of an area and spot an unusually large garden that is sufficiently large enough and has direct access onto the road. Look to make enquiries with the Local Planning department, but in the first instance here are a few basic provisions to help you assess if the plot is suitable.

You may find whilst searching that there an unusually large space between houses and that the numbering sequence has missed out a number, this may have been done intentionally by the officers in the council some years back when arranging the street numbering as they considered the space large enough as an 'in fill' plot and made an allowance.

Another, potential plot is where a house has spare land to the side, enough to comfortably pass with a car and a very deep garden, somewhere in the area of 100m. If you spot that other gardens have been built on in a similar way in that particular locality, this is called 'back land' development and as long as the potential dwelling, (usually single dwellings) does not appear to be incongruous i.e. out of keeping, you may be able to develop it. You must ensure that the donor house retains sufficient parking and amenity space. Most planning departments use a guide of between 18 and 21 metres separation between 2 dwellings.

For every house, you should ensure that you have at least 2 off street parking spaces (some Planning departments will indicate that new houses close to town centres, do not require off street parking within the curtilage of the site). You will need to site the house no further forward than 'other' adjacent houses, this is known as the building line. A typical 3 bedroom starter home will have a footprint in the order of $40m^2$ so, around 8mx5m or 6mx6.5m each semi, that sort of general size, so if you can position a box of this size on the plot, allowing for it to be set back similar to the house adjacent and ensuring that there is sufficient land remaining for 'amenity' or garden space, usually 10.5m from the rear of the house. You may have found yourself a plot for a single dwelling. If you can fit double this footprint on the plot i.e. 10 x 8 - $80m^2$ you may have found yourself a plot for a pair of semi-detached 3 bedroom houses.

Your next move is to run the numbers to ensure it all stacks up. There are a number of 'self build' magazines out there. At the rear sections they list typical regional build costs. Using this as a guide you can estimate the build cost based on the square metre area of your project. Your local research should determine how much a 3 bedroom semi should achieve on the market allowing for an element of profit. When taking the build costs away from the potential value and allowing an element for profit this will give the value of the land to you.

For example:

Potential market value of 2 x 3 bed semis: £160,000 x 2 =	£320,000
Build cost 80m² (per house) x2 = 160m² x £1100/m²	£176,000
Design, planning, Building regs and legal fees	£ 10,000
Element of profit on costs say 20%	£ 40,000
Total costs	£226,000
Residual land value (max)	£ 94,000

The land value of £94,000 is the maximum you should pay, remember that at this stage you are buying a garden and will need to obtain planning permission and secure the land on an 'Option" (Refer to Options in Chapter 2) and pay an option fee, so try and offer the least as reasonably possible. Remember you will be doing the hard work to get permission, any saving will go to your bottom line profits. From the owner's point of view, if you succeed they will get a windfall and because they are selling part of their private residence the money they receive will be tax free.

As land is not currently in high demand, you may be able to find a pair of plots with Planning permission, you may choose to either undertake the project purely as a developer, in which case you will need to allow for your tax obligation based on your profits. However if you feel that you could persevere for the next 4 years or so, living a nomadic life style you could do this exercise any number of times allowing 9-12 month build periods per development and make a non-taxable profit of every time, and I would hasten to bet, that once you did the first one the second and third would cost you less, as you will have (hopefully) established a good relationship with the builder merchants and builders and picked up a few tricks of the trade to help you drive costs down. For example, if you chose to build the same designed houses, your architectural fee's would drop as the only change to the plans would be the site plans. The house design could stay the same.

I often use the same 3 bedroom semi house plans that I designed some years ago, if I do a project such as this. I just need to ensure that the plot is a least 16m wide and 24m deep, which allows for an attached garage. If the plot is only 11-12m wide I need the site to be a little deeper to accommodate 2 cars on the front parked bumper to bumper, another 5m is ideal making a 30m deep plot.

To fund this as individuals you may be able to get funding from the specialist self build funders such as the 'Build Store'; a quick search on-line will show some results. These funders will often provide funding of 60-70% of the land vale and then 60-70% of the build costs, so well worth exploring.

Another way for you to proceed once you have completed the first property and ready to move into the second, is rather than sell it, is to take a BTL mortgage out, by doing this you will only be able to recover 70% of the value, but the timing is more under your control as you won't need to find a buyer and wait for them to pay you. You could apply for a BTL mortgage a month before you complete the build and arrange for the money to be drawn down to help fund the next project. Often the 70% funding will cover all your costs, but I must admit it would be better to get the sale as the other 30% which may well be £48,000 will ease your journey tremendously. Perhaps consider the BTL option after you have built the third unit.

CHAPTER 14

Case Studies

Chapter 14. Case Studies

Penfilia Road - Auction Purchase

I bought this house in 2011 and interestingly it was not the one I had intentions of bidding on. I had renovated a house in another town and a house on the same street was on the auction list; having done one in the street and realised a sale, I knew exactly what the maximum bid was. Someone else bid over my maximum of £33,000 so that was the end of that. However, another lot was announced and I noticed that the auctioneer was struggling to sell it and he got as far as £50,000 saying that 'he was unable to sell at that price and if anyone was interested to speak to him after the auction'.

From my knowledge, this type of property in that area would sell for around £85-90k, so £50,000 for 2 bedroom house was attractive, and knowing that I can totally refurbish a terraced house for under £25,000 it was worth a look.

After the auction had ended I offered £52,000; the auctioneer advised that he would seek the vendors instructions and I left the auction. An hour later he called to advise that the offer had been accepted. I agreed to go into the office the next morning and sign, but asked that I meet someone prior to this at the property so that I could give it the once over. Providing the house wasn't subsiding or totally wrecked there was a profit of £15-20k to be made.

Now I wouldn't advise that you buy a property without seeing it, especially at the beginning of your journey, but as I mentioned, my local knowledge and experience of refurbishing gives me a lot of confidence in these circumstances.

Another aspect of this property was that the vendor had gained Outline Planning Permission for a bungalow on the rear garden which had access from a road to the rear! The agents advised me that it had been previously for sale for £29,995, which was a little strong, as it was still on the same title the vendor had asked if I was interested in buying that as well. I wasn't really interested in a plot in that area, especially at £30k so initially and genuinely declined, however the agents persisted and asked "what I be willing to pay", I avoided making any offers and asked what the vendor would take. The agent advised that the vendor would be willing to accept £70,000 for the house and plot. Again I really wasn't interested in buying it for £18,000, so again I declined stating that I wanted to concentrate on the refurbishment. At the viewing of the property the next morning, the agent persisted and asked what would I be willing to pay. At this stage I began to see some potential as I knew I could build the bungalow for £60,000 and it would be worth in the region of £100,000, so I replied by saying I was willing to pay £60,000 for the house and plot. (£52,000 for the house and £8000 for the plot). By the time I had arrived a the agents office to sign the contract, to my surprise I was advised that the vendor accepted the £60,000 and the deal was done.

The property had been owned by an elderly couple, I believe one partner had died and the widow was selling having moved out to live with family, so it really needed modernising, typically the ground floor had two rooms with a kitchen to the rear in an extension which was approximately 25 years old, so built with building control involvement. There was some rising damp issues, nothing major so an injected DPC was installed and as always we hacked off the plaster up to one metre and re plastered with a salt inhibitor. I installed an RSJ in order to make the two rooms into one large lounge and whenever I refurbish a house rather than waste money spending time rubbing down and trying to make skirtings and architraves look better, I simply rip them all out, including the door linings. I install new linings, doors, architraves and skirting boards. This instantly improves the appearance for not a lot of money. I will often replace window boards and stair balustrading so all the joinery looks fresh and clean.

The kitchen was replaced as was the bathroom with new clean neutral colour tiling. I will buy a nice bathroom suite with glass shower screen and I will always install a shower over the bath whether it be a shower valve or a bath mixer tap with shower fitting. Introducing an electric shower can be costly as you will need to install an RCD on the fuse board and run a 6mm electric cable from the fuse board to the bathroom.

Prior to completing the property and installing new fencing and some decking to the garden to cover the dated and scruffy looking patio I had to excavate in the rear garden and connect a foul water drain for the bungalow.

Here is a nugget of information. The drainage searches undertaken had shown that there was an adopted sewer running through the garden and along the rear of the houses, which is what I had expected, only the adopted sewer will be shown, the private drains are not. The private drains are the drains around a property that connect to the main.

If I wanted to connect into the main sewer I would need to make an application to the Water Authority and in some areas connections to a main sewer can only be done by 'approved' contractors, so you would be looking at £1500-2000 for the connection. BUT, by connecting to the drains that leave the donor property 'prior' to connecting the 'main' you avoid the complication of involving another contractor and save a packet. My ground workers, under my supervision and hands on involvement undertook the excavation and the connections.

Once we back filled the excavations we levelled the garden and laid new turf.

The property went into the market at £89,950 and I accepted £87,000 after 6 weeks or so. The refurbishment costs were £12,000.

Summary.

Purchase cost £52,000
Refurbishment costs £12,000
Legals and sales agents £3500
Sale price £87,000

Profit £19,500

Auction tip.

I'm sure that you have heard many times not to get caught up in the excitement of an auction and go over you maximum.

My procedure at auction is once I've set my maximum I sit back and wait, I don't let anyone know I'm bidding on a property and do not bid until the auctioneer has slowed the bidding down and starting to say things like 'it's here to be sold' and 'I'll take another £500 if it helps' providing this is within my budget. If it is within my budget I won't come in until everybody is done bidding against themselves and the auctioneer says 'going once'.

At one auction I attended with the view of buying a large plot of land, which had planning permission for a pair of houses. My maximum bid was set at £130,000. As mentioned I sit tight and let things run, the bidding started at £70,000. I'd learned from the agents that there were a number of private individuals interested in buying as a large plot for one house so I was confident that they would drop out at around £85,000 but they pushed on into the 90's, so it seemed that it was going to end up at around £110,000. It appeared that it was down to 2 people bidding against themselves and it was at £105,000. Looking good I thought!

Then it got to £108,000, then £109,000 and slowly got to £120,000 when another bidder stepped it! Bugger! I thought, And, I hadn't started yet. So these two took it to £127,000 and it stalled...one chap had shook his head and did not want to go any further, then "going once" was heard at which point I confirmed my involvement with a quick 'flash' of my number to get the auctioneers attention and said "£128,000" the other bidder came back after a few moments delay, with £128,500 so it was in my turn at £129,000, the other chap, after another delay returned with £129,500, so I was now at £130,000, my maximum. I felt the other guy was faltering, But would a bid of £130,000 do it? I wasn't confident, so I shouted "£132,000". The room fell silent and everyone was looking on the direction of the other guy. He shook his head to confirm that he was out.

That bold move knocked the guy out and the plots were mine. I know it was £2000 over the budget, had the other chap come back with a bid of £133,000 I was out, but £2000 in the scheme of things on a project worth £560,000 worth of sales was a small premium to pay. I would only need to add a £1000 to the price of each the houses when they completed nine months later. I was really chuffed with myself.

Old Road.

I bought this house in 2002 and it was the house that really enabled me to expand and grow the portfolio.

I had made an appointment to visit a customer who wanted an extension on their house, and after the visit I noticed a house for sale on the same road, it was a typical terraced house and on the 'For Sale' sign was a 'Priced Reduced' board. This immediately caught my attention and I called the agents. I was advised by the sales agent that the house was on at £29,995, but was reduced due the 'problem with the front wall'. The agent invited me to go to the office to read the Structural Engineers report on the condition of the front wall of the house.

Typically of a Structural Engineers the report was very detailed and he had recommended that the front wall be taken down and rebuilt due to a 'bulge' that had occurred in the centre of the wall this would involve propping up the floor and roof and carefully taking down the stone wall to the front, the wall would need to be taken down to the foundation and rebuilding from there up. To be honest this problem is common but I have never seen a house opened up as he recommended. The recommendation in my view was incorrect and he advised that the cost of the work would be £10,000

To explain, in South Wales main front and rear walls of terraced house houses are constructed of 22 inch thick stone walls (500mm), these are effectively two skins of natural stone each 200 odd Millimetres thick and the gap between filled with the rubble. Over time the two skins can start to move apart (delaminate) with the centre of the movement being located below and between the first floor windows and the top of the ground floor window and front door. If this movement is not arrested it can continue upward and sideways and start to affect the whole front wall and spread to the adjacent properties.

As mentioned the Structural Engineers had recommended rebuilding of the wall at a huge cost and the sellers were expecting to reduce the price by that amount. This was like Christmas Day and my Birthday arriving together. This amount of £10k was completely over the top and I had calculated in my head that I could have done this for less than £5000. But not only that, from my construction knowledge, there was another way of repairing the wall and far cheaper again.

My enquiry with the agent found that the sellers were the 'church' who at one time owned the whole terrace and, as they were not a private seller, I took advantage of the fact that the person acting for the church would be 'disassociated', so I offered £18,000 and the offer was accepted.

Once I had the keys I arranged for a builder I knew, who had previously undertaken the task I needed him to do and set about the repair to the front wall.

The method I used is known as 'Lateral Restraining' and undertaken as follows.

The floor boards in the area of the front bedroom adjacent to the front wall are removed to expose the floor joists, the floor joists were checked for any infestation and rot and treated as necessary with timber treatment.

Timber noggins are installed the same timber section as the joist between the joists, i.e. 200x50mm, off set 200mm from the front wall and securely fixed. 14-16mm holes are drilled through the noggins and into the stone wall ensuring that the drill enters the outer skin for a minimum of 150mm. The drill holes in the stonework are injected with a special resin and a 12mm threaded bar is inserted into the resin filled holes and left overnight to set.

The next day toothed washers and nuts are added to the threaded bar and tightened onto the noggins. This method has now anchored the section of the outer skin that has previously moved back to the floor joists providing the support. To finish the work and to add further support the floor boards are replaced with 2440x1220mm (8x4) 22mm Plywood sheets and these are fixed into the joists with 38mm screws at 150mm centres bonding the whole area of the floor and wall together.

This work including materials and labour was around £700. I spent further on the house which included redecoration, installed a new kitchen, which I fitted myself and new carpets. The total expenditure was £2500.

Once I had introduced tenants I applied for a mortgage; the surveyor made no reference to the front wall and I received a valuation of £57,000. I released 85% on a BTL mortgage which netted me £47,000 after fees and legals.

The following week I went shopping and bought 3 more properties and if I recall I bought my wife a pair of Kurt Geiger shoes with matching bag.

Ritson St.

I found this property by calling into one of my local estate agents and speaking to the manageress who I knew well. I had decided to do the rounds of the agents and see what was potentially available. I'd called into the first agents and there was nothing of interest, I returned to the car and drove the quarter of a mile or so to the next street where the other estate agents are grouped together, both the first agents and the others are located on one way streets and parking on the street where they are grouped together is limited. I was unable to find somewhere to park so I thought 'Oh I'll call some other time' but then I thought 'No Mike you're here now, drive round the block again and find a space'. So I did and parked off the Main Street and walked to the agents. I was really happy that I did.

It's strange but this happens a lot, I'll walk in and say my hello's to the staff and sit down and ask if there's anything that may be of interest to me, and initially I always hear, 'no nothing really, nothing we can think of'. And then when I look around and start probing it's only then that they say, 'Oh yes, that's been on a while, they'll look at an offer' and 'Oh, what about this' etc.

On this occasion, the manageress asked if I'd been to the auction the day before that they had run, to which I replied I had not, I had simply missed it. She went on to say that a terraced house didn't receive any bids and it had a guide price of £32,000. It was a typical 3 bedroom terraced house that would go back on the market when refurbished at £87,500. She advised that there was a crack inside and that as a result the bedroom window wouldn't open and close properly! There was a problem with the front wall!

Now that didn't sound right to me, so I agreed to see the house the next day, we went straight to the said problem and I hummed and ah'd and suggested that it wasn't a problem for me. I offered £30,000, and the offer was accepted.

From experience I know I can 'gut' a typical terrace property and refurbish it for around £25,000 not including a new roof, so this was right up my street. The crack and the window issue were nothing to be concerned about, the fault that the agents were focusing on, the crack and the window were not related at all.

When confronted with a crack, the first consideration is where it is located, is it where two walls join? if so which direction is the crack opening up. If say the rear main wall has a rear extension abutting it at 90 degrees and the crack is wider at the top than the bottom, then the extension is pulling away from the house, and was not properly tied into the main wall when constructed. In this case the crack was uniform in width and whist evident on the first floor did not extend down to the ground floor, it was located where the party wall meets the front main wall, but if it were a structural problem where the front wall was moving away from the party wall, the crack would have extended right through the wall, ground floor through to the first floor and would be wider at the top, but it wasn't. This was nothing to be concerned about and the problem with the window was purely limited to the opening casement, the two defects were not connected. The agents were incorrectly focusing on these defects making more of it than it was and it was putting purchasers off.

I stripped the house, ceilings, wall plaster and internal partitions. We installed a steel beam across the middle of the house to make the two ground floor rooms into one to open up the house. The crack which was mainly evident in the plaster was still in the stonework, so we removed all the mortar to the stone work in the area of the crack and re-pointed the whole area approximately 200mm either side and prior to re plastering fitted a 450mm wide sheet of stainless steel mesh over the whole area of repair. By adding the mesh, if in the event that there were any slight movement in the wall the render and plaster which adhere to the mesh would not crack again.

This refurbishment included installing new UPVC windows and doors, a new staircase and balustrading, new first floor timber partitions, new kitchen, bathroom suite and tiling and new internal doors and joinery. My total expenditure was just under £20,000. The property went back on the market with the agent that introduced me to it. This is always the way I do it, I promise that any agent who introduces me to a property that I am going to refurbish always has it back to sell for me.

As the agents know the house, anytime during the work anyone who makes an enquiry for available properties the agents can refer to my house in the knowledge that when it's completed it will be like new.

Once the house was finished I had an offer on it for £85,000 within a week, which I declined and I agreed a sale of £86,500. Had the property been for sale for a month or so and the £85,000 was the only offer I would have taken it, but I considered that the offer made within the week was from a keen purchaser and felt that they would improve on the amount offered. Having sold many properties you just get a feel for the strength of your product and the market place at the time. So take the money and move on to the next project.

Wern Rd.

You may have heard property investors saying they can save money during a phone call. Well here's how I saved £10,000 in a phone call by asking the right questions and being congruent.

These two houses came to me via an associate that I do business with, he knows what I do and when undertaking some repair works for one of his clients, the clients asked him if he knew anyone who would be interested in buying two houses. He was a 'tired' landlord who did not live local to the houses and typically when there are issues to be dealt with the properties become a drain, even though he only lives 40 minutes away!

My associate told the vendor that he would contact me and enquire, he made the call to me describing the properties and the circumstances, he said that he would be working in one of the houses and invited me to call in on him and have a look around.

They were detached 3 bedroom houses; one had been tenanted by a family for 12 years or so and the other had been recently vacated. My associate advised me that his client wanted £100,000 for the two!

I did some research prior and found that these detached houses in that particular area were rare, the area was typically terraced and semi-detached Local Authority properties. When I researched the values a typical terraced or end terraced value within half a mile was around £85-90,000. Therefore I was confident that these properties that I was being offered would easily be worth £100,000 each when in a good condition.

At the viewing the property that I had access to was a bit rough but let-able. The other I didn't see but heard the several dogs barking in the house and the state of the material being used as curtains hanging in the windows gave me an idea of what the tenants were like.

So I confirmed my interest, and later my associate called me with the telephone number of the vendor. I called the vendor who seemed very pleasant, no nonsense type of guy who knew that he had a problem selling these houses, especially with the 'Adams Family' in one of them. So we got on well from the start, my associate had obviously told him that I don't beat about the bush and do what I say I'm going to do.

We discussed the properties and he confirmed that he was looking for £100,000, I asked him what rent he had been receiving and he replied sheepishly, £65 per week each! These should be at least £110 per week so I asked why . Well, he said "they live like animals there, so I have just left them to it for the past 12 years". I told him that I would usually expect to receive £100-105 per week for house that costs me £50,000 and that clearly I need to spend some money to improve these houses to get a reasonable rent. Implying that these houses weren't worth £50,000 based on the income.

There was a moment of silence and then he said, "Ok I'll take 90 for the two, I won't go any lower than that".

Well, I wasn't going to argue with this, I knew I could refurbish each for around £25k, at £45,000 they would at most stand me £75,000, so I happily agreed to buy them for both for £90,000 and suggested that we meet at the properties.

A week or so later we met, shook hands and I confirmed that I would instruct my solicitor. A number of weeks later when we had a completion date agreed, I suggested that we meet again at the properties to inform the tenants of the tenanted house that I would be taking over. When I got there, he was waiting outside and I was informed that the "Adams Family" had moved into next door as it wasn't in such a state as their house! "Oh" I said, "I wasn't expecting that!" My plan was to re decorate that house and look for a new tenant to rent it at £110 per week.

Then the vendor said, "Here are the keys I've got to go, I'll leave it to you, good luck, I'm going on holiday for 2 weeks" got in his car and drove off!

We hadn't completed, the completion was due 10 days after.

I spoke to the tenants who were on LHA (benefits) and told them that they would need to apply to the benefits and increased their claim, which in fairness they had no problems with as the mother and mature son would be able to claim £55 each.

I then had to consider, that I would now need to refurbish the house they were in and Oh, what a state! Can you imagine, mother and mature son, 3 daughters running back and forth and 4 dogs. The carpet was...well I'll leave it to your imagination, and the Bathroom!

Then the mother said, "My other son is looking for somewhere, is it ok for him to move in?" I asked if she was sure, and she said that he stays on occasions so he knew the house well. So, I agreed to meet him and he said that he was happy to rent it and it was close to his mother ! I told him that I really needed to improve the house, so if it was ok with him I would start the renovation works whilst he lived there and I would accept £70 per week. He was able to claim this amount form the LHA, so everyone was happy.

From my point of view I was immediately into positive cash flow earning £780 per month.

I started the renovation works on Property A after 2 months and in the 3rd month I learned from the guys on site that the tenant has been rehoused by Her Majesties Prison service! To be honest this suited my guys on site as they could really get stuck in instead of working around him, and his dog!

I completed the refurbishment three months later, so over 6 months in total and about 2 weeks prior to completing it, I applied for a BTL mortgage. I provided the mortgage company with a Word document explaining the works and a series of photographs showing the work as it progressed together with a spreadsheet showing the costs of the works. This totaled £28,000 materials and labour.

On my mortgage application form I requested £115,000 and the valuer agreed to it, I spoke to him and explained my reasoning why I applied for £115,000, his response was that he had no problem with my figure, he was impressed with the quality of the works and had no issue with 'my' valuation request.

I had found recently a property locally that was on the market for £120,000 which was the highest in the area on the market at the time; he would also research in this way and look for recent sales.

I find that with valuers, you can't influence them, but if you apply for as amount that is 'reasonable' and you can show comparable prices locally he is more likely to go with you.

There is the thought that if you apply for more he can always 'knock it down', but you don't want him knocking it down below what you really want. So, I try and keep it reasonable.

Once I was in the last month of the refurbishment a local couple knocked on the door and asked if they could rent the house, I agreed to visit them at their home to interview them and to get a feel of how they would treat my newly refurbished property, and to my pleasant surprise the house was better than I had expected. It was spotless in fairness and I did not have a problem in letting the property to them and payment terms were agreed, £130 per week - £563 PCM (£6756pa)

Shortly after they moved in, I 'mentioned' that I was going to have to refurbish next door, as there was a lot of money 'locked' into it, the 'Adams' family knew that I could not do all the work that they had seen me do next door whilst they lived there. One day the mother asked me if I was going to do the work, I said that I would be at some time.

The next thing I heard from my builder was that they suspected that they were on the move, as they had seen boxes coming and going. I was on holiday at the time and by the weekend they had moved out completely. Tenants always leave what they can't carry, but in this case they removed everything, they even removed the carpets and burnt them in the back garden. They didn't leave a light bulb either!

An inspection of the house confirmed that it would need improving, but not to the level of next door. At the time of writing that work was in progress, dry lining of the walls on the first floor, a complete redecoration, new kitchen and a strip out and refit of the bathroom suite. I envisage a spend of around £8000.

Summary

Property A.

Purchased price £45,000
Legals £1500
Refurbishment works £28,000
Valuation £115,000
Funds released £86,250
Cash out £11750
Gross Development Profit £40,500

Property B.

Purchase price £45,000
Legals £1500
Refurbishment works £8000 (Budget)
Valuation £110,000 (Expected)
Funds releasable £82,500
Cash out. £28,000
Gross Development Profit £55,500

Mike's top tip!

Perseverance and determination are key, you must never get complacent, you must be committed and keep searching for the right deals.

CHAPTER 15

Glossary of terms

Chapter 15. Glossary of terms.

All In. A mix of sand and small grade hardcore used for preparing concrete

Ball Valve A fitting used in plumbing pipe work; where it is used, the flow of water can be isolated via a small screw head (rather than a tap)

Blinding A sand layer, usually laid over hardcore in preparation for the DPC, to prevent the DPC being punctured by the sharp stone.

Cut Roof Normally found in older properties where the roof has been constructed from individual timbers leaving a usable void/space.

CLS (Canadian Lumber Standard) softwood cut from fast growing pines making it suitable for the building trade purchased in lengths of 2.1- 4.8m and used in the construction of stud partitioning, joist and rafters.

DPC Damp Proof Course. A plastic material available in 100-600mm wide rolls and used as a layer in a wall construction to prevent moisture rising. The wider materials can be used in a variety of ways.

Eaves. The collective name for the components where the base of the roof meets the walls, the soffit, fascia and gutters

Flashing. A length of lead usually between 150 and 300mm used at the junction of a roof and a wall or abutment.

Fascia. The element of the lower part of a roof to which the gutters are fixed.

Gutter. A plastic or metal trough to collect water from a roof.

Gable. The triangular shape of wall above Eaves level at the end of a house. Also known as Gable end and Pine End

Hip Iron. A metal 'L' shaped component used in the construction of roofs to retain a hip tile. Used where a roof is Hipped as opposed to having a gable.

Hipped roof. A roof where there are 3 or 4 slopes.

Hardcore. Graded Crushed stone used in the construction of new floors 15-25mm.

Lintel. A concrete or Steel component used to form the top of an opening.

Membrane. A plastic sheet usually 1200 grade used as a component in the construction of a new concrete floor.

Mortar. A sand and cement mix used to bond brickwork and blockwork.

Noggins. Short pieces of timber placed between floor or ceiling joists to provide support or additional fixing.

PSE. Planed Square Edged, a term given to regular timber used in carpentry and joinery.

Pad stone. A solid concrete component placed in a wall and used to place an RSJ onto to displace the load through the wall.

Purlin. A timber component used in the construction of a 'cut roof' placed to support a rafter.

Rafter. A timber component used in the construction of a roof that forms the outer shape to which the roof covering is fixed.

Render. The term given to a sand and cement mix applied to walls.

Gully. Rain Water Gully - a drainage component that collects rain or waste water and discharges into the drainage system.

RSJ Rolled Steel Joist - A structural steel beam seen as an 'I' section. used to replace structural walls.

Splicing. When a new piece of timber is added to a joist or rafter to replace a rotten or damaged section.

Scarfing. When a new piece of timber is added to a skirting or architrave to replace a rotten or damaged section.

Soffit. The horizontal surface material to the underside of the Eaves.

Self Levelling Screed. A powder-based product mixed with water to enable an uneven floor to be levelled. For use between 2 and 12mm.

Screed. A sand and cement mix used over a concrete slab to provide a level surface. (with fibres for use with underfloor heating)

Trussed roof. The timber structure that forms the roof, a pre-made frame designed by specialists.

Treated/Tantalised Timber. This is timber that has been impregnated under pressure with preservatives such as Creosote to prolong the life of the timber and to protect it from decay.

Verge. The sloping edge of the roof where it overlaps/ meets the gable wall.

Weyroc Board. A 2400x600x22mm board with tongue and grooved edges. Usually used in the construction of new houses or to replace a larger area of individual floorboards.

Wall ties. A metal component used in the construction of cavity walls used to hold, 'tie' the two skins together.

CHAPTER 16

Frequently Asked Questions

Chapter 16. Frequently Asked Questions

Q. Can I get a Buy To Let mortgage from a High Street Bank?

Some High Street banks do have a specialist lending team, but in general a BTL mortgage broker will have access to all the mortgage products available at any given time, these products regularly change so it is advisable to make enquiries as to what BTL products are currently available.

Q. Should I take a fixed rate mortgage or a tracker mortgage?

Most lenders will have a product that has both a fixed rate and a tracker rate, often the interest rates are very similar. They will be described as being x% over base. These products are often for between 2 and 5 years, so your choice will depend on how the market is at the time, currently with the potential interest rates rising within 2 years, you may want to go for a fixed rate deal. During the years where the interest rate was falling Tracker mortgages were more attractive.

Q. I want to buy a house to refurbish and flip, can I get a BTL mortgage.

Providing the house is what is known as 'readily let-able' you should be able to secure a BTL mortgage, but as these products are approved on the basis of the property being rented and the mortgage repayments being made from the rents received, you will need to ensure that you are able to cover the mortgage. Also usually these products tie you in for 2 years, if you sell the house within the term you will have to pay a redemption fee, which is often 2-3% of the loan.

Q. What funding is available to buy a property to flip?

There are specialist lenders who provide what is called bridging finance, the loans usually being between 60-70% of the purchase price or valuation, whichever is the lower. The cost of these facilities are more expensive by way of arrangement fees and interest rates and must be repaid in full usually within 12 months.

Q. Can I rent out my own house if I move into another house.

Yes, and you should write to your residential mortgage company advising them and request their permission to let. They may well increase the interest rate, so the decision whether to tell them is up to you.

Q. Can I buy a house with money from credit cards?

Yes, depending of course on the amount of credit you have available and the price of the house. It is possible to buy houses in certain areas for around £40,000 and have an equal amount of credit available via one or a few cards. You will need to have a card that enables you to transfer money to your bank account and I would suggest one that has a 0% transfer rate for 12 months.

Q. I have a poor credit score. What tips would you give me that can help me to improve my score?

You should regularly check your score, if you have any errors you should write to credit file companies explaining the matter. If people are included that you are no longer associated with, an ex-partner for example you should write them a letter of 'disassociation' giving them dates etc. Make sure that you do not miss any payments whether it be your mobile phone contract or a catalogue. Make sure that you keep the number of applications for credit within a 3 period to no more than 2 or 3. If you have credit card accounts that you no longer use or need, close them. Ensure that you are on the electoral register. To increase your credit score, make regular purchases on a card or cards and pay off the balance in full every month, your car fuel or shopping for example.

Q. I have had a bad experience investing in property and had my fingers burnt already. What advice would you give me if I wanted to give it another go?

If you got it wrong first time you probably didn't have enough knowledge of property investing or property letting; like anything the better prepared you are the better chance you have of succeeding. If you fail to prepare, prepare to fail. Get educated, learn from someone who has experience. Invest in your education - it will pay dividends.

Q. Sometimes, when I view properties, I find it hard to think objectively about the purchase. What advice could you give me to help me to think more objectively?

Property investing can be very exciting, there is not much in the world that the ordinary person can buy and make money from it. Finding a property and then viewing it with the intentions of buying is fun, but you can get caught up in the moment, so before you view make sure that it satisfies all of your criteria, whether for renting or flipping before you arrive. The purpose of the viewing is to ensure that it is worth the money it is on the market for, and if not you either make a lower offer or walk away. The more properties you view, the more confident you will become in realising what is right for you.

Next steps...

I truly hope that you have been inspired by reading this book; my aim was to provide you with an insight into my world and to show you that investing in property, when done with the correct knowledge can change your wealth status, your future and that of your children. Whilst remaining in full time employment you can build a profitable portfolio and achieve profits of £20,000 - £50,000 from one refurbishment project taking less than 6 months.

With expert guidance and instruction from me you can learn how to make a business out of property and become a property millionaire in under 5 years.

If you are serious about your future, and you recognise that you need to make a change in your life, you must take action.

Property and Refurbishment Master Class

During the Master Class I will give you expert advice and detailed explanations of all the aspects of property investing and show you real examples of the various projects I have undertaken.

You will learn:

How to find and assess suitable properties for refurbishment to flip, Buy to Let or HMO's
How to make accurate financial assessments during your viewings
How to prepare a schedule of work
How to appoint tradesmen and purchase materials at the right prices.
How to manage your project cost effectively
How to prepare your project for sale or rent
How to arrange finance for your purchase
How to re-finance once complete extracting the maximum possible.

You will also receive a work book on arrival which includes all the course content for your use and to retain after the course.

For details of my Property Master Class please go to: **www.mikewoodsthepropertyexpert.com** for details of courses.

VIP Platinum Personal Mentorship Program

A 9 month VIP Platinum Personal mentorship program is available to you. Following an initial appraisal meeting you will receive a structured action plan based on your personal financial circumstances to ensure that you SUCCESSFULLY Invest in property, you will also have unlimited access to all the Master Class events. In addition, you will have the opportunity to have exclusive mentoring sessions at Trullo Monte d'oro in Puglia, Italy.

Please go to **www.mikewoodsthepropertyexpert.com/VIPprogram** for further details.

13671061R00114

Printed in Great Britain
by Amazon.co.uk, Ltd.,
Marston Gate.